COLNIÆ
DELINE
N
O
M
K Capella
M Camera Communis
N Domus Capitularis
O Bibliotheca
Q Capella

LINCOLN CATHEDRAL

A JOURNEY FROM PAST TO PRESENT

LINCOLN CATHEDRAL

A JOURNEY FROM PAST TO PRESENT

Philip Buckler + Gavin Kirk + Nicholas Bennett + Mary Lucas + Anne Coltman

THIRD MILLENNIUM PUBLISHING, LONDON

LINCOLN CATHEDRAL

Editor's note

I first saw Lincoln Cathedral on a bright, blowy day in May 2009. With the sun pouring through the windows, it struck me as an extraordinarily light and open place. Since then I have visited the cathedral in many different weathers, but no matter how dark the sky outside, the feeling of lightness and welcome remains. It has been a pleasure and a privilege to get to know this wonderful building and the people who are part of it, most especially the writing team: The Very Revd. Philip Buckler, The Revd. Canon Gavin Kirk, Dr Nicholas Bennett, Dr Mary Lucas and Mrs Anne Coltman. Creating a book of this kind depends upon the kindness and help of many others as well. Particular thanks must go to John Campbell, who was so generous with his time, to Anne James for coffee, cake and her patience on the parking front, to David Wheelband, Lynn Snelson, Sally Crawford and Jo Makin , and, of course, to Phil Crow and Dick Makin, who between them took so many of the remarkable photographs in this book. I am grateful also to Neil Burkey for additional picture research, and especially to Susan Pugsley for a design that brings text and images together to such striking effect. This book will, I hope, be a tribute to them all, as well as to the cathedral itself.

Pamela Hartshorne

Above: high on the cathedral, exquisite details like this newly-carved grotesque are unseen by most human eyes.

Previous page: Lincoln Cathedral soars above the city and the surrounding countryside.

CONTENTS

INTRODUCTION

THE VERY REVD PHILIP BUCKLER, DEAN OF LINCOLN

From past to present, from medieval times to the modern day, people journeying to Lincoln have seen the majestic Cathedral Church of the Blessed Virgin Mary standing dramatically above the flat landscape. Its towers can be seen for many miles around, encouraging pilgrims on their way and assuring the people of Lincolnshire of God's continuing presence in his world.

Approached from the south or west, the cathedral rears up at the top of the escarpment above the Witham and Trent valleys. There it stands, watching over the city of Lincoln that nestles below it. From the north or east its three towers appear on the horizon, a reminder of God the Holy Trinity to whose glory the cathedral is built.

It is a place full of surprises. Although from a distance this remarkable building looks all of one piece, closer inspection reveals a mixture of styles. Its appearance is massive, but it displays a delicacy that delights. Inside it seems vast, yet it offers an intimacy to those willing to engage with it. Built of Lincolnshire limestone from the cathedral's own quarry nearby, like every cathedral it is also made up of 'living stones' – the people who, down the ages and into our own day, work and worship here. Currently staffed by almost 100

The dean's verger takes an altar frontal from the vestment chest to prepare the nave altar.

Opposite: view from the central tower, looking west out over the Lincolnshire countryside.

Opposite: the nave filled with worshippers at Christmas.

people, it enjoys the support of nearly 500 volunteers who willingly share their skills, knowledge and love of this place with all who visit.

Originally built as a symbol of political and religious power, it dominates all around. But times change, and today's understanding recalls the origins of *dominus* in the teaching of Jesus as the Lord who came to serve. So the cathedral today seeks to serve the people of the city and diocese of Lincoln as well as the countless pilgrims drawn here from across the world. It also plays its part in the wider Anglican Communion. Lincoln Cathedral is the seat of the bishop of Lincoln and a centre of worship and mission.

Kings and queens have spent time here, saints and sinners all have a share in its history. Those attending Evensong each day hear read out the names of people associated with the cathedral down the centuries who are remembered on the anniversary of their death, including Peter Barbo, prebendary of Sutton cum Buckingham, who was finally crowned Pope Paul II and who died on 26 July 1471; Matthew Parker, prebendary of Corringham, dean of Lincoln and later archbishop of Canterbury, who died on 17 May 1575; and George William Welbourne, carpenter then verger, who died on 9 August 1951. Following each evening's remembrance is said the prayer that St Hugh laid down for the daily use of his canons:

> *Almighty and eternal God, you are Lord of both the living and the dead, and have pity on all those whom you know will be yours in faith and works: we humbly beseech you, that those for whom we have determined to offer our prayers, whether the present age yet holds them in the flesh or the age to come has already received them out of the body, may, of your merciful goodness, come to pardon of all their sins and so be held worthy of eternal joys; through our Lord who lives and reigns with you in the unity of the Holy Spirit, God for ever and ever. Amen.*

In Roman times Lincoln stood at the meeting point of two great roads, the Fosse Way and Ermine Street. Today Lincoln Cathedral stands as a meeting point of time and eternity, a place of deep holiness and welcome refreshment for pilgrim and visitor alike.

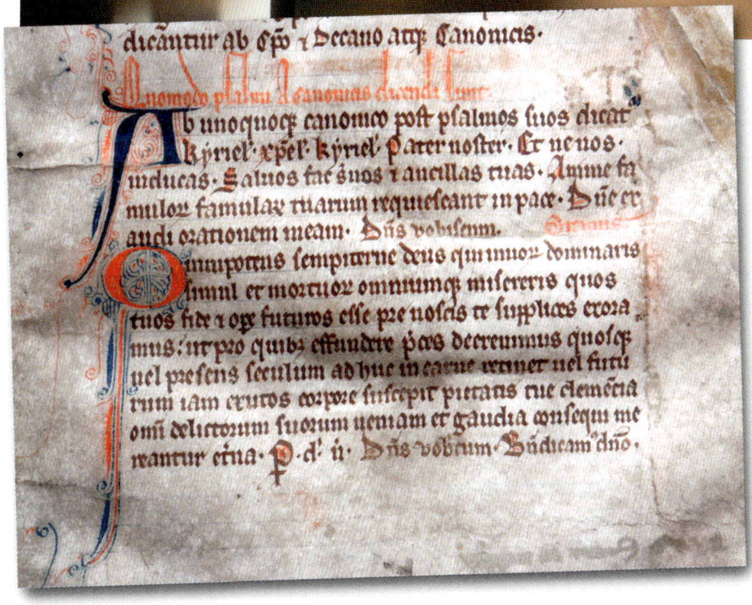

dicantur ab epo & decano atq; canonicis.
Quomodo psalmi a canonicis dicendi sunt.
Ab unoquoque canonico post psalmos suos dicat
Kyriel. xpel. kyriel. Pater noster. Et ne nos.
inducas. Salvos fac servos & ancillas tuas. Anime fa
mulorum famularum tuarum requiescant in pace. Domine ex
audi orationem meam. Dominus vobiscum. Oremus.
Omnipotens sempiterne deus qui vivorum dominaris
simul et mortuorum omniumque misereris quos
tuos fide & opere futuros esse prenoscis te supplices exora
mus: ut pro quibus effundere preces decrevimus quosque
vel presens seculum adhuc in carne retinet vel futu
rum iam exutos corpore suscepit pietatis tue clementia
omnium delictorum suorum veniam et gaudia consequi me
reantur eterna. P. d. n. Dominus vobiscum. Benedicamus domino.

This book invites you to make your own pilgrimage around the cathedral, appreciating its beauty, recalling its history, sensing its sacred and mysterious nature and meeting some of those 'living stones' – the people who themselves are a part of Lincoln Cathedral today.

Vergers use walkie-talkies to communicate with each other.

St Hugh's Foundation Prayer in the 13th-century Liber Niger.

1 SETTING AND HISTORY

SETTING AND HISTORY

BY NICHOLAS BENNETT

Previous page: detail of carving on the Norman doorway at the West Front.

Opposite: the cathedral rises out of the autumn mists like the heavenly Jerusalem.

Below: Lincoln Cathedral held in the hand of its founder, Remigius. Detail from the Remigius Window.

Lincoln Cathedral stands majestically, like the Psalmist's vision of the City of God, set on His holy hill. On an autumn morning, when the mists lie low over the river, the traveller from the south might see the sunlit church seeming to rise out of the clouds, an image of the heavenly Jerusalem. The origins of the cathedral, however, lie not in apocalyptic revelation but in the more secular concerns of earthly kings.

The ecclesiastical map of 11th-century England was the result of the fluctuating fortunes of its rulers. In the south of the country, where the control of the kings, first of Wessex and then of England, was strongest, the dioceses were small and compact, allowing the bishops to exercise an effective pastoral oversight of their flocks. In the north and east, however, those parts of the realm that had been most affected by Scandinavian invasion and settlement, royal authority was much less secure, and this was reflected in the size of the dioceses. Some of the Saxon bishoprics had disappeared during the Danish invasions: that of Lindsey (north Lincolnshire) ceased to exist in the 870s, and the bishop of Leicester was forced to abandon his flock and flee to Dorchester-on-Thames in the 890s. The counterattack of the English out of Wessex in the early decades of the 10th century reshaped the political landscape but did little to change the ecclesiastical boundaries north of the Thames. Over much of the Midlands the Church continued to be ruled from Dorchester. The reappearance of a bishop of Lindsey during the course of the 10th century may reflect the ambition of the archbishops of York to expand their influence southwards. They incorporated neighbouring Nottinghamshire after 956 and were still claiming Lindsey at the end of the 11th century.

The lack of success by the late Saxon kings in reshaping the ecclesiastical landscape reveals the tenuous control they had over the northern part of their kingdom. In contrast, the dukes of Normandy worked closely with the Church, the boundaries of whose jurisdiction matched closely those of the duchy. As king of England, therefore, William I, the Conqueror, would have quickly seen the importance of using the Church as a means of strengthening his authority, particularly in the north. Rumblings of discontent in that region began soon after the Conquest. In 1068 Edgar Aethling, a rival to the throne, left the king's court and fled to Scotland, while the earls Morcar and Edwin also went north, bent on rebellion. William therefore undertook what has been described as a 'military promenade', building castles at Warwick, Nottingham and York on his way north, and at Lincoln, Huntingdon and Cambridge on his return south. The castle at Lincoln was established within the walls of the upper Roman city, with its 'motte' strategically placed at the southwestern angle.

11th-century walrus ivory seal matrix of a papal legate [The Collection, Lincoln].

Despite the presence of these powerful symbols of Norman authority, two more rebellions broke out in the following year, the second combining English opposition with the arrival of an invading force from Denmark. William's prompt suppression of these risings was followed by his terrible devastation of the north, so thorough that years later the Domesday survey recorded village after village as 'waste'. There were to be no more rebellions during William's reign. He now acted to strengthen his hold on the strategically vulnerable area around the Humber estuary, where so many Scandinavian armies had invaded the land. In 1072 he ordered the bishop of Dorchester, the Norman Remigius, to transfer the seat of his diocese from its southerly location to Lincoln, one of the most thriving cities in the kingdom and situated at the heart of the northern Danelaw. A writ announcing this decision was sent to all the sheriffs throughout the extensive diocese, emphasizing that the move was made by the advice of the pope and his legates. A walrus ivory seal matrix, discovered in Lincoln in 1985, is thought to have belonged to the papal legate Hubert, who is known to have been in England in 1072. Its presence here may be the result of the negotiations behind the transfer of the bishop's *cathedra* to the city.

The king's writ also gave Remigius land on which to build the new cathedral, and here, in the southeastern quarter of the upper city, he set his craftsmen to work. By the time of his death in May 1092 the church was ready for consecration. As Henry of Huntingdon memorably described it, Remigius built a strong church in a strong place and a beautiful church in a beautiful place. The West Front in particular, perhaps incorporating the episcopal residence, encapsulates the power and authority of Norman rule. At the same time its three colossal arches lay claim to the continuity of the new regime with Lincoln's Roman past. The building of Lincoln Cathedral served as a reminder that the Norman Church and the Norman kings were here to stay.

The identification of the west end of Remigius' building as the bishop's residence serves as a reminder that to begin with the cathedral was staffed by his household. Bishop and canons were regarded as a single entity, and gifts of land to endow the new foundation were made 'to bishop Remigius and his canons' or 'to God and the church of St Mary of Lincoln and bishop Robert'. This unity of structure can also be seen in Domesday Book, where the prebendal estate of Welton is listed among the lands of the bishop.

There were, however, fundamental strains pulling at this unity of bishop and chapter. The former had an extensive diocese to rule, and, although he could delegate some of his work to archdeacons or other deputies, there were some functions – confirmation, ordination, the dedication of churches and churchyards – that only he could perform. Bishops also served as royal advisers, and he would therefore need to spend some time at court. This peripatetic life contrasted sharply with the fixed responsibilities imposed on the cathedral clergy. The daily round of prayer and praise required the presence of at least some of their number in Lincoln. The completion, adornment and maintenance of the fabric of the building needed to be supervised. Not least, the cathedral chapter was responsible for the government of the expanding community of vicars, clerks and lay staff that was growing up around the new foundation.

This increasing separation can be observed in the charters of the cathedral. By 1146 it was necessary for the pope to issue two documents, one confirming the possessions of the bishop and the other those of the chapter. In 1160 Bishop Robert Chesney granted to the prebendaries of Lincoln exemption from episcopal jurisdiction. This new independence of the chapter is illustrated by the use of its own seal, of which an early example can be dated to around 1150. It can also be seen in the provision of houses in the cathedral precinct for the residentiary canons.

Exchequer Gate and the cathedral beyond. On the left in front of the gate is the church of St Mary Magdalene, which replaced the original St Mary's on the cathedral site.

On Palm Sunday 1185 the cathedral building suffered serious damage in what was described as an earthquake. Inspired by the leadership of the saintly Bishop Hugh of Avalon, the chapter began to rebuild on an altogether grander scale. The death of St Hugh in 1200 and his canonization 20 years later brought pilgrims to Lincoln in increasing numbers, so that no sooner was the new building complete than the chapter determined to pull down the east end and replace it with the magnificent Angel Choir in order to provide their saint with a fitting shrine.

This work may have been inspired by the leadership of successive bishops, notably St Hugh himself, but it was the chapter that was responsible for the day-to-day management of the building campaign, and by the early 13th century some members become more than mere names. Dean Roger of Rolleston, originally a clerk of Archbishop Baldwin, was brought to the diocese by St Hugh himself; he held office for nearly 30 years. His successor, the Somerset-born William of Thornaco, was noted for his piety; when he left office in 1239 he entered the Cistercian Order at Louth Park Abbey where 'he spent his leisure in steadfast prayer and contemplation with Mary at the feet of the Lord'. Precentor Geoffrey of Deeping, trained as a clerk in the household of St Hugh, directed the liturgy of the cathedral for nearly 20 years. He bequeathed to the chapter a magnificent glossed Psalter, still in the cathedral library. The great teacher William de Montibus brought distinction to the office of chancellor; the scholar Alexander Neckam described him, in a typical play on his surname, as a 'steadfast mountain and pillar of the faith' who adorned successively the mountains of St Genevieve in Paris and St Mary of Lincoln and finally attained Mount Zion in heaven.

The statutes drawn up during the 13th century to regulate the rights and responsibilities of the members of the cathedral body tell us much about the daily liturgical life of the foundation. They enable us to trace the key role of the precentor in supervising the conduct of the services ➤ p.22

THE CLOSE

BY MARY LUCAS

The cathedral is surrounded by a particularly fine group of buildings in the close. They are medieval in origin, though many now have Georgian or Victorian façades. They provide a beautiful, tranquil setting and enable many of its staff to live within a stone's throw of the cathedral.

After the eastern extension of the cathedral in the 13th century breached the city wall, it threatened the security of the clergy as they attended services at night from their homes in the close, so the buildings were enclosed within a 12 foot high crenellated wall. There were six gatehouses in the circuit of this wall, which were locked and guarded at night. The most impressive of the two surviving ones is the massive three-storey inner Exchequer Gate, just west of the cathedral. The blocked openings at ground-floor level are the remains of the original shops built within it, a unique survival of this feature. The outline of the three great arches, elaborately vaulted and decorated with religious imagery, mirrors those on the Romanesque centre of the West Front. Entering the precinct through this gateway provides an awe-inspiring view of the cathedral, especially at night when the building is so splendidly illuminated. It marks the symbolic entrance to the peace and sanctity of the cathedral where the pilgrim leaves behind the hurly-burly of everyday life beyond the gate.

Gardener Albert Richardson working in the close in the 1960s.

Potter Gate is another 14th-century gatehouse, in the southeast circuit of the close wall, though it is now marooned in the middle of the road with traffic going round both sides of it. To the north stands Priory Gate Arch, a 19th-century rebuild of the medieval Northgate gatehouse. Three other medieval close gates have been demolished, although a postern still spans Greestone Stairs, the steep pedestrian ascent from Lindum Road to Minster Yard.

The whole area remained enclosed until the 18th-century turnpike road ran through the close and the dean and chapter gave up their right to lock the gates. The road around the cathedral was lowered, and the area around it was made more accessible to traffic – a situation that Pevsner, in 1989, lamented as 'a scandalous state of affairs'.

THE HOUSES

Of the various types of old buildings in the close, formerly all owned by the cathedral, the most impressive are the dignitary houses, the homes of the dean, subdean, precentor and chancellor. These came into cathedral ownership mostly in the 13th century as gifts of the original inhabitants and were established as permanent dignitary residences.

The east side of Minster Yard, including the house where William Byrd lived, 1562–73 (see plaque on p.90).

All that remains of the huge 12th-century deanery that was built on the south side of Eastgate is part of its north wall – it was demolished in 1847 by the then dean, who had a new house built on the adjacent site, now part of the Minster School.

The 13th-century subdeanery, now the Cathedral Centre, stands in Minster Yard opposite the southwestern corner of the cathedral. It was greatly damaged during the civil wars of the 17th century but retains its stone façade with its distinctive front bay window of 1491.

Between it and Exchequer Gate was the residence of the precentor from 1270 to 1960. It, too, was much altered following the civil wars and has medieval features and even a Roman hypocaust. It is currently the subdeanery.

The chancery at 11 Minster Yard, which recently became the deanery, has the most striking exterior of the dignitary houses. It was built in the 13th century and served as the chancery for nearly 700 years from 1321, when it was enlarged and its extant chapel added. It is the only building in the line on the east side of Minster Yard to retain its medieval façade, of *c.*1500. This beautiful frontage is an early example of brick with stone quoins and windows and is unique in Lincoln, enhanced by its symmetry and central oriel window, with a carriageway to the extensive buildings behind.

Early chancellors did not always reside in Lincoln, and during their absence or the vacancy of their office this great house was let to other canons and, most famously, from about 1381 to Katherine Swynford, then mistress of John of Gaunt who had many connections with the city and cathedral, until her marriage to him in 1396. Their eldest son, Henry Beaufort, became bishop of Lincoln, and after Gaunt's death in 1399 Katherine returned to Lincoln to live in the Priory (2 Minster Yard), another grand close house, occupied mostly

The Deanery door, detail.

Close houses at the West Front.

View across Minster Yard to Vicars' Court (left), the Precentory, and Cantilupe chantry.

by treasurers and other canons until the 17th century. Built against a surviving stretch of the close wall, the Priory stands back from the line of houses in Minster Yard. It retains some of its original 13th-century features but is much restored. Its name dates from its Victorian incarnation as a private girls' school, and it is now part of the Minster School.

Several other canonical houses survive, such as those at 12 and 13 Eastgate, now the homes of the bishop and the chancellor, and Deloraine Court (4, 5 and 6 James Street) the oldest and longest inhabited of the surviving canonical houses, which has Romanesque pillars in the cellar.

THE CHANTRY HOUSES

Until the Reformation several other close houses housed groups of chantry priests who lived communally. These buildings were given by the founders of the chantry who funded up to seven priests to say daily masses for their souls at a specific altar in the cathedral.

Next to the old deanery, northwest of the cathedral, stood the large courtyard building that became the works chantry in 1321, after the chancellor moved to his mansion at 11 Minster Yard (see above). The role of its priests was to pray for the donors to the cathedral 'works' in the chapel in the southwest transept. It was let to laymen after the dissolution of the chantries in 1547 and was demolished in 1828, in a 'ruinous condition'. Over a century later the resulting empty space was utilized as a static water tank to quench any potential fire in the cathedral during the Second World War. Fortunately, it was never needed and is now hidden under a pleasant green surrounded by railings.

Two other chantry houses have retained their original names. Burghersh Chantry in James Street, a large house with two medieval halls, became a chantry house in 1346, housing five chantry priests and six choir boys. Two more priests and two boys of the Buckingham Chantry lived in its gatehouse. (Apart from the house, the name lives on in the choir boys and girls being known as 'Burghersh chanters', except for the four senior ones who are choristers.) A disastrous fire in 1964 destroyed much of the medieval fabric of this house, which is now a truncated version, with its medieval hall fireplace standing rather forlornly in the garden behind.

Cantilupe Chantry in Minster Yard was built by Sir Nicholas Cantilupe in 1355. He also built the adjacent house in 1366 to house seven priests, whose chantry altar is at the northeast end of the Angel Choir. The southern part was 'Gothicized' in the mid-19th century to give it a more picturesque appearance, but it retains its medieval fabric. It is now the precentory. The northern house, which is occupied by the dean's verger, looks out on to the green where once stood the Church of St Margaret, which was given to the cathedral by Henry I in 1115 and was where its baptisms and marriages took place until its demolition in 1780.

VICARS' COURT

On the eastern side of the green a gateway leads into Vicars' Court. Here the vicars choral, deputies of the often absent canons, lived communally. Built during the early 14th century, the range is the earliest surviving vicars choral building in England. This quiet quadrangle, hidden away behind a two-storey gatehouse with a vaulted carriageway and a porter's lodge, contained 25 individual lodgings, with a room and a garderobe for each vicar and a common stair for each pair (an arrangement that was later adopted at Oxbridge colleges). There were also a chapel, hall and kitchen, and much of the original fabric survives. The southern range has dramatic views over the city. The corporation of vicars was dissolved in 1934, severing the connection of the priest vicars with the court and allowing laypeople to rent the lodgings.

THE NUMBER HOUSES

In contrast to all these grand medieval stone houses, the row of much smaller, elegant brick houses to the west of the cathedral dates from the early 18th century, a 'tidy' replacement of their medieval predecessors, which housed an assortment of cathedral workshops. They are known as the 'number houses' because they were reputedly the first ones in Lincoln to have numbers instead of names.

CLEARANCE AROUND THE CATHEDRAL

The desire to improve the view from his house led to a local resident, Mr Alfred Shuttleworth, who lived at Eastgate House (now replaced by the Lincoln Hotel), to demolish much of the buildings to the north and east of the cathedral in 1892, opening out the view from the north. The demolition included eight medieval houses on the south side of Eastgate and Priorygate and College House, next to the Chapter House, which had served as the chancellor's school from 1400. A wish to demolish the Wren library as well was fortunately thwarted. The resultant space now has the bronze statue of Alfred, Lord Tennyson, the Lincolnshire poet laureate, on it.

Consistency of ownership for so many centuries ensured that this remarkable group of buildings survived, albeit in changed form. Our knowledge of their former appearance is in many cases possible because their picturesque appearance attracted various artists who sketched them.

Left: Priory Gate in the early 19th century [Lincoln Cathedral Library, Willson Collection].

Right: entrance to Vicars' Court from Minster Yard.

and the duties of the vicars choral who were appointed to sing the offices in the place of the canons. They take us through the liturgical round, starting with the preparation of the altar before vespers, the censing of the tomb of Remigius afterwards, leading on to compline, matins, lauds, the day-bell, peal and morrow mass, prime (for which sailors would customarily ring on Christmas Day), the little hours of terce, sext and none, the arrangements for processions on double feasts, high mass with the censing of the choir and the tombs, and finally back to vespers. We are left in no doubt that worship was regarded with the utmost seriousness, as being the fundamental reason for the cathedral's existence.

By the 14th century, when the chapter acts and accounts become available, we not only know the names of the canons but, in many cases, can also identify the houses in which they lived. The building of the close wall after 1285 gave a physical expression to the sense of community among the cathedral body, and this was enhanced by the provision of specific housing for the vicars choral, poor clerks and choristers. On coming into residence, a canon would ask for a vacant house to be assigned to him. This might not, however, be one of the best houses, because the senior canon had the first choice of a vacant property, and the new canon might well be offered one of the less desirable residences to begin with. There was thus always a certain amount of movement in the close, as canons gradually rose in the scale of seniority and transferred to ever more desirable residences.

When Katherine Swynford rented the Chancery during the 1380s her neighbours in the close would have included some 12 canons keeping residence, the Keeper of the Altar of St Peter (the chapter's principal legal officer), the priest celebrating at the shrine of St Hugh, with his chaplain, deacon, subdeacon and eight singers, two principal shrine-keepers with their chaplain and clerks, the day-keeper of the shrine with his clerk, two night-keepers, the vicars choral, four clerks, the choristers, the succentor, the sacrist and his clerk, the clerk of the common, the chapter clerk, the clerk of the fabric, the masters of the Grammar and Song Schools, the master masons and carpenters, two thurifers, the organ blower, the door-keeper of the close, the candle-lighter, the sweeper, the bell-ringers, the candlemaker, two clerks 'who rouse the people' (could these have been fundraisers?) and the clerk 'who brings the dove'. When the collectors of the poll tax surveyed the close in 1377 they found a total of 129 men in holy orders of some degree, and even the few lay inhabitants were connected to the chapter by ties of employment and service.

The cathedral building grew ever more majestic, its three spires rising into the heavens. Meanwhile, its clergy joined with other benefactors to adorn its worship with costly plate, jewels and vestments. An inventory drawn up by Treasurer Henry Litherland in 1536 lists chalices and thuribles, chests and pyxes, crosses and candlesticks, chasubles and copes, with details of their decoration and often a note of their donors. There was a great chalice, the gift of William of Wykeham, bishop of Winchester and 'some time archdeacon of Lincoln', the founder of New College, Oxford; it bore images of the passion and resurrection of Christ, with the salutation and coronation of the Blessed Virgin. There was a silver and gilt feretrum (portable shrine), made in the form of a church with a transept, a steeple in the middle and 20 pinnacles, with images of the Virgin at one end and of St Hugh at the other, given by Treasurer John Welborne along with other magnificent donations, among them the choir stalls. There was, too, a great image of the Virgin, crowned and holding a sceptre, her Child sitting on her knee, holding an orb, with the arms of the donor, Precentor Mason, at his feet.

All of this beauty and craftsmanship was swept away four years later when the commissioners of King Henry VIII visited the cathedral and loaded all the treasures they could find on to carts, to be carried off to the royal treasure house. The shrine of St Hugh, the very reason for the building of the Angel Choir itself, was destroyed. The world of the old religion was under attack. In 1534 the cathedral clergy had already sworn allegiance to the king as head of the Church in England, rejecting henceforth the authority of the pope. Then, after the accession of King Edward VI in 1547, the whole elaborate structure of the medieval liturgy, the central purpose of the cathedral's life since its foundation, was dismantled. In its place came the English Prayer Book, substituting the two services of Matins and Evensong for the continuous round of prayer and praise that had echoed

Opposite: view through Exchequer Gate to St Mary's church.

Queen Elizabeth I playing the lute in a miniature by Nicholas Hilliard.

around the cathedral day by day for centuries. The cathedral choir was in danger of losing its role altogether, as it was enjoined 'to sing henceforth no anthems of our lady or other saints but only of our Lord and then not in Latin but shall turn the same to English, setting a plain and distinct note for each syllable'.

The future for English cathedrals looked dark, as reformers urged that they should follow the monasteries and chantries into dissolution. Their canons were idle and unprofitable, spending their substance in 'superfluous belly cheer', argued Archbishop Cranmer. A later writer condemned cathedrals altogether as 'dens of loitering lubbers', where dean and vice-dean, canons and petty canons, chancellor and treasurer ('otherwise called Judas the pursebearer'), singing men and squeaking choristers, organ players, readers and vergers 'live in great idleness and have their abiding'. The brief Catholic reaction under Queen Mary during the 1550s brought a measure of respite, but the accession of the Protestant Queen Elizabeth in 1558 and the return of the extreme reformers from exile in Calvin's Geneva, eager to establish the new Jerusalem in England, boded ill for the future.

That cathedrals survived was due in part to the stubbornness of the queen, more conservative in religious matters than she appeared to be and, like her father before her, determined to stay in control. It was also the result of the skilful way in which two successive archbishops of Canterbury – Matthew Parker and John Whitgift (both of whom had earlier served as dean of Lincoln) – steered the Church of England on a middle course between the two extremes represented by the Catholics and the reformers. The cathedrals themselves, however, still needed to find a new role.

The new bishop of Lincoln in 1559, Nicholas Bullingham, was one of the Marian exiles, a man whose reforming credentials were impeccable. Determined to use his authority to cleanse the English Church of any pre-Reformation survivals, he nevertheless found at Lincoln a cathedral chapter that refused to change. The dean, precentor and chancellor had all been appointed in Mary's reign, and, although they accepted the Elizabethan settlement, their sympathies were with the Catholic past. Bullingham did succeed in introducing a reformer into the chapter. This was the archdeacon, William Todd, who came into residence in 1560. Like many of the reformers, he was a married man, and he brought his family to live in his house of residence in the close. The queen herself disapproved of the marriage of the clergy, especially those serving in cathedrals, and she issued a proclamation forbidding the residence of clergy families in cathedral closes. It is not difficult to imagine the satisfaction with which the other members of chapter (all unmarried) recorded in February 1562 the order that Todd remove from his residence his wife and the other women of his family.

It was no doubt the conservative majority on chapter that was behind the surprising appointment in March 1563 of the young William Byrd as Organist and Master of the Choristers. One of the greatest musicians of his age, Byrd must have already shown such promise that despite

his youth (he was in his early 20s) he not only secured the post but was given a total salary of £13 6s 8d, making him one of the highest paid cathedral musicians in the country. He was also Catholic in his religious views. In later years he was openly a recusant, refusing to attend the services of the established Church, and throughout his career he wrote music for the Roman rite. This would not have worried the chapter of Lincoln in 1563, and Byrd set to work with plenty of youthful energy and enthusiasm. In this he was assisted by an order of the government (in which the hand of the music-loving queen herself can be detected) that cathedrals should continue to maintain singing men and choristers to perform 'modest and distinct song' wherever appropriate in the liturgy. It was the genius of Byrd and his contemporaries that seized this opportunity to lay the foundations of the unique Anglican choral tradition that remains one of the glories of English cathedrals. Despite some teething troubles, as when the Puritan John Aylmer joined the chapter in 1564, vowing to purge the cathedral of 'that nest of unclean birds', William Byrd succeeded in laying the foundation for a growing repertoire of music to be sung in the choir at Lincoln.

Tensions persisted, however, between those who upheld the Elizabethan settlement and those who continued to press for further reform. The success of the Puritan party in securing the appointment in 1584 of a divinity lecturer to expound three times a week in the cathedral did not meet with universal approval; there were those who said that 'they desired as much a tale of Robin Hood as to hear him preach'. The reformers continued to grow in influence, however, and the very position of bishops came under threat. Petitions were laid before Parliament to banish from the Church all such who served only 'to puff up too corrupt and wanton flesh'. Nationally, matters came to a head with the outbreak of civil war in 1642. In the following year Parliament finally succeeded in abolishing both bishops and chapters. For the first time since the late 11th century the community of Lincoln Cathedral was disbanded. In place of the daily offerings of sung worship, Puritan preachers delivered lengthy sermons. Where craftsmen had

The choir leads carols by candlelight.

Rare books in the Wren library.

created beauty in stone, wood and glass, soldiers smashed carvings and windows with axes and hammers. For 17 years the building lay neglected and decaying.

The Restoration of the monarchy in 1660 brought with it the return of the chapter to the cathedral. The new dean, Michael Honywood, and his colleagues set to work. They undertook the repair of the fabric, the adornment of the interior and the restoration of the musical foundation. Confiscated endowments were painstakingly regained. A new library was built, its shelves filled with Honywood's own priceless collection. In Lincoln, as all over England, cathedrals took their place once more in a revived national Church. The strength of feeling for this symbol of Lincoln's civic identity was revealed in the extraordinary scenes in September 1726 when a local mob rioted in protest against the chapter's proposal to remove the spires from the western towers.

From the 17th century the number of residentiary canons was fixed at four – the dean, precentor, chancellor and subdean – and as a result many of the houses in Minster Yard were occupied by the laity. Surviving letters give a flavour of life in the 18th-century close. An outbreak of smallpox in May 1745 caused panic: Mary Thoroton packed her daughter off to stay with friends at Coleby, while the subdean and his family 'are in the greatest of hurry to be gon'. In happier times there were dinner parties, cards and music, or the evening parade on Minster Green, 'the Mall of this place'. A summer party at the deanery in 1796 included 'a little concert consisting of a French horn and four or five other instruments below stairs for the amusement of the sitters by'. Mary Yorke, the dean's wife, thought that Lincoln people had but three ideas ('eating, going to Church and card playing'), but there were other diversions, such as the races, while the building of the Assembly Rooms in Bail Gate in 1745 brought the county society into the city.

Although the Georgian chapter is scarcely remembered for its energy, the canons by no means neglected the cathedral fabric. The inspired choice of James Essex as architect ensured that the new work – corner spires and battlements on the central tower, a new bishop's throne and reredos in the choir – blended harmoniously with the old. The cathedral's music, however, was in a poor state. A visitor in 1791 heard the litany sung by two lay vicars 'with voices like bulls', while half a century later the music was described as 'sluggishness and torpor personified'. A new broom was needed, but little could be done as long as a bishop like George Pretyman saw the chapter as a means of providing for his own family. An apocryphal story tells of the bishop's wife saying to her

Bailgate.

The head of Dean Butler is carved on the entrance to the cloister from the library, opposite that of William Gladstone.

DEAN BUTLER: A MAN OF INFLUENCE

BY PHILIP BUCKLER

Of the many individuals who have contributed to the life of the cathedral, Dean William John Butler deserves particular mention. Of his time as dean (1885–94) it was said: 'The cathedral services might be admired for their musical effect, but any attempt to represent the cathedral as a spiritual force and activity would have been received a few years ago with a smile.' The nine years Butler spent as dean transformed the spiritual life of the cathedral.

His earlier years at Wantage, where he had exercised a devoted ministry influenced by the Oxford Movement and people such as John Keble, had seen a blossoming of spiritual awareness and the foundation of a religious community. He kept his links with the Wantage Sisters when he moved to Worcester and thence to Lincoln.

His emphasis on the prayer and worship offered in the cathedral led to a pattern that has since developed into the daily services of our present time. He improved the furnishings, and it is recorded that on his 70th birthday he helped to lift the marble slab on to the new High Altar. He brought back into regular use the side-chapels around the cathedral and began to use the retro-choir as a place of worship. Today that area is being re-ordered to develop its use as a sacred space for both public and private prayer.

In the present Deanery are bookcases given to Butler by all the curates he had trained at Wantage. Their names are recorded in brass plaques, among them names such as H.P. Liddon and W.C.E. Newbolt, both later to become canons of St Paul's Cathedral.

Dean Butler died in office on 14 January 1894 and is buried in the cloister garth. A memorial effigy in the retro-choir was dedicated in 1896. Its Latin inscription pays tribute to one who was a wise, single-minded, strenuous shepherd of souls.

The carol service on Christmas Eve is one of the biggest services of the year.

John Matthew Wilson Young, Organist and Master of the Choristers 1850–95.

The kindling of the Easter Fire on Easter Eve.

husband, 'I hear the poor chancellor cannot last long,' to which the bishop replied, 'Then we must get George out of the navy'. George Pretyman Jr did indeed become chancellor in 1814, and his brother Richard was appointed precentor three years later. They remained in office, resistant to change, until the 1860s.

The second half of the 19th century saw the gradual restoration of the spiritual life of the cathedral. A new organist, John Young, began to raise the standard of music. Chancellor Massingberd introduced Sunday afternoon services in the nave. The pace of change accelerated with the arrival of the monumentally learned Christopher Wordsworth as bishop in 1869. Wordsworth aimed to restore to the cathedral something of its medieval sense of purpose, appointing Edward White Benson as chancellor in order to found a theological college. The spirit of improvement culminated in the deanship of William John Butler. For nearly 10 years he brought to the life of the cathedral his

wealth of experience as an energetic parish priest. He introduced additional communion services on Sundays and festivals, with a weekday celebration on Thursday mornings. He added a Sunday evening nave service. When a critic compared Sundays in Lincoln Cathedral with Clapham Junction, he took it as a compliment.

Much of what was achieved during these years followed from the desire of Chancellor Massingberd and others to make the cathedral useful to the city and diocese in which it stood. This challenge has continued to inspire their successors in the 20th century and beyond, as the building has welcomed increasing numbers from all over the world, the fabric has benefited from a regular programme of maintenance, the musical tradition has reached new levels of excellence, and the work of education and scholarship is handed on from generation to generation. English cathedrals represent one of the major successes of the Church today. Remigius would be agreeably surprised.

A PLACE OF PRAYER

BY PHILIP BUCKLER

In May 2007 an IT consultant from Lincoln, Peter Moore, was one of five people taken hostage in Iraq. Throughout the time of his captivity prayers were said in the cathedral. A candle was kept alight, symbolizing the prayers of many not only from Lincoln but across the world. It also kept alive the flame of hope for those who watched and waited. When asked for what we prayed and hoped, the dean would say simply: 'One day Peter Moore will be able to come to the cathedral and extinguish the candle himself.'

On 30 December 2009 Peter Moore was finally released, the only one of the Iraq hostages to be returned alive. In a quiet but profoundly moving ceremony on 26 January 2010 Peter Moore did come to Lincoln Cathedral and extinguished the candle. The faithful prayers of many had been answered in the way for which we had hoped.

The dean and Peter Moore at the ceremony.

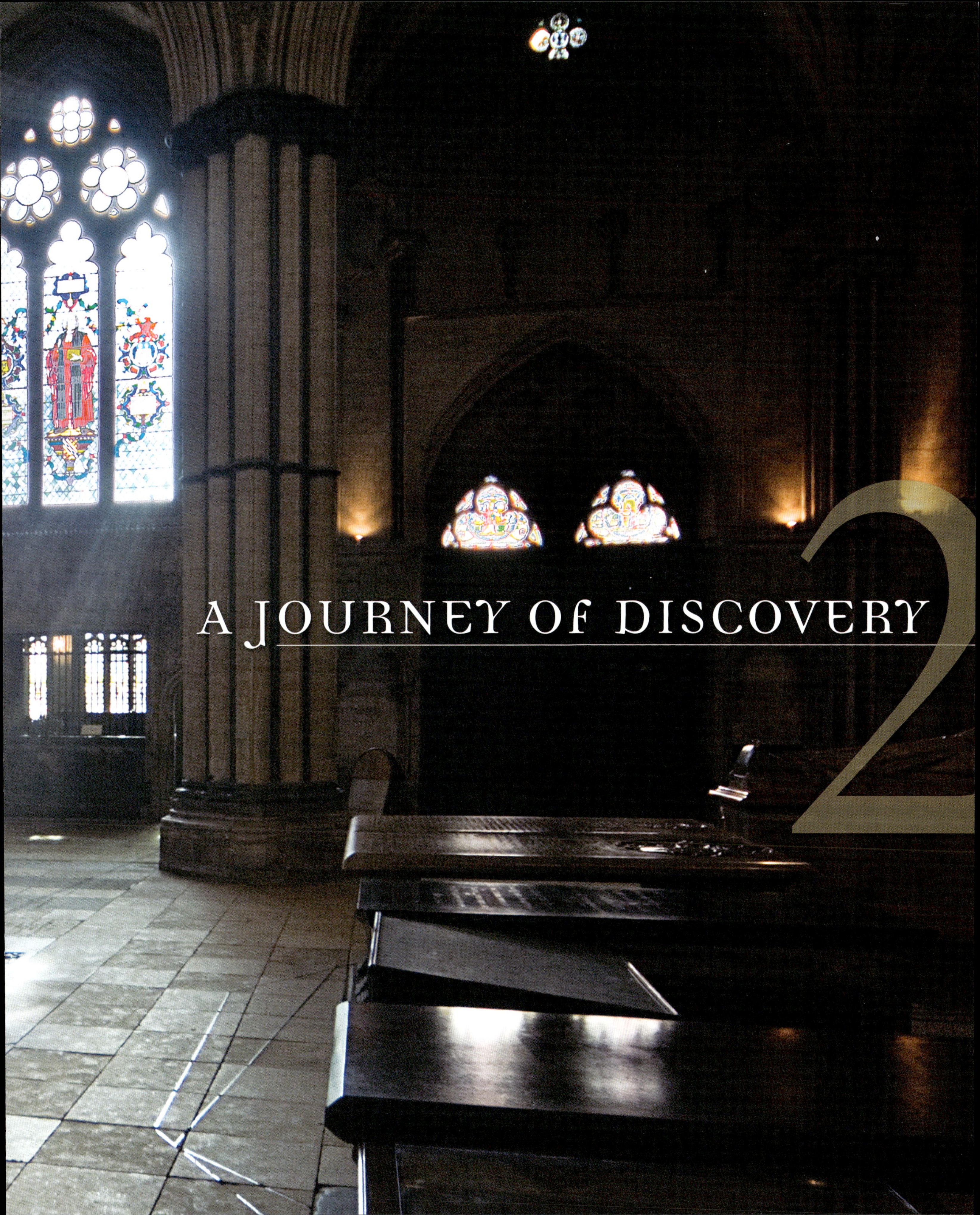

2 A JOURNEY OF DISCOVERY

THE WEST FRONT

BY ANNE COLTMAN

Previous page: a moment of reflection for a duty chaplain as light streams into the Angel Choir.

Below: reconstruction of the 1092 cathedral by David Vale.

Distant views of the cathedral alert the mind to the presence of a large, imposing building. Not until the visitor emerges from the deep arches of Exchequer Gate does the great West Front burst on the eye, just as a miraculous set appears as the stage curtain rises. This dramatic elevation is a vast frontispiece concealing the glorious spaces of the cathedral church and the fruits of over 900 years of Christian witness. Set behind this façade, as if supporting it, are the two west towers, and at its outer angles two large turrets materialize from the elaborate arcading and culminate in pinnacles, themselves the size of many parish church steeples. The west elevation dwarfs the close houses that fan out from Exchequer Gate but also provides them with unrivalled views of medieval architecture. A fascinating insight into the cathedral's architectural history from the Norman and Gothic through to the 20th century is revealed in the development of the West Front. The West Front provides the first impression of the diocesan cathedral to the worshipper and visitor, a fact that would never have been far from the minds of the medieval creators

Shortly after the Norman Conquest William I established a castle in Lincoln that embraced the area of the Roman upper city. In 1072 a council held at Windsor determined that episcopal sees should be in walled towns and not villages. Lincoln was the town chosen to become the focus for Bishop Remigius' huge diocese, so removing the seat from Dorchester-on-Thames, a relative backwater in the southwest corner of his diocese. He began his new cathedral between 1073 and 1075, positioning it within the castle enclosure, a model familiar to him from Fécamp and one offering security. The cathedral's earliest fabric can be seen in the West Front, which still retains part of this 11th-century building, dedicated, although perhaps not completed, in 1092.

The 11th-century work can be recognized by the simple, unadorned masonry surrounding the three tall, deep entrance recesses and the big arched niches to their north and south, the form reminiscent of a Roman triumphal arch. Recent research suggests that Remigius constructed a large, squat, tower-like building with substantial walls and features derived from secular architecture, giving it defensive potential. As well as its western wall, parts of the north and south walls are still visible in St James's Chapel at the rear of the Morning Chapel and in the Ringers' Chapel, but the eastern wall has gone, replaced at the centre with a large arch opening into the nave. ➤ p.36

Opposite: the West Front today.

BISHOP REMIGIUS OF LINCOLN, 1067–92

Remigius was a Benedictine monk from the Abbey of Fécamp, one of the most important monasteries in the duchy of Normandy and situated within the castle ramparts. Its importance is underlined by the frequent visits from William of Normandy, who celebrated his victory over King Harold there in 1067. His date of birth is unknown, but he was probably in his 30s at the time of the Norman invasion of England. If an inscription on a lead plate found in William de Aincourt's tomb outside the West Front of the cathedral is to be believed, Remigius was related to the de Aincourt family and in some way to William himself.

The chronicle of Henry of Huntingdon says Remigius was at the battle of Hastings, and other sources suggest that he supplied ships for the invasion. William's victory was the springboard for Remigius' career. In 1067 he was consecrated to the bishopric of Dorchester-on-Thames, the largest diocese in England, and immediately took up a place among the elite. The early years of his bishopric were not without incident, and in 1070 he was suspended because his consecration was deemed uncanonical. He was accused of purchasing his bishopric and of making extensive contributions to the Norman invasion. In 1071, however, Remigius was in Rome with Archbishop Lanfranc, through whose personal intervention he received absolution from Pope Alexander III for the flawed consecration and was reinstated. This was but one example of the complex political machinations of the time, and Remigius was politically astute. This awareness may account for his actions, in particular his extreme care not to give any opportunity for the archbishop of York to claim the diocese of Lincoln for the York province.

Surprisingly, the Norman administration made no attempt to divide the diocese, perhaps because there was no wish to provide a case for York to claim the northern part. By April 1073 plans to move the seat of the diocese to Lincoln had been sanctioned by the pope, part of a general move to establish bishoprics in towns rather than villages. The transfer was a great administrative achievement in highly charged times. The most tangible result of the move was the building of a new cathedral in Lincoln. A Norman castle had been built there in 1068–9, and the cathedral was begun in

The Battle of Hastings in a detail from the Bayeux Tapestry (1073–82).

Remigius holding the cathedral, in a detail from the window dedicated to his memory.

the mid-1070s. There is some doubt as to the exact form of the first cathedral church. The three central bays of the West Front we see today may have been its west end, but possibly this part, in its first incarnation, was part of Remigius' own residence in the form of a fortified tower, with the cathedral church further to the east. Remigius died in 1092, the day before the new cathedral was dedicated.

In addition to his building of 'a strong church in that strong place, a beautiful church in that beautiful place, dedicated to the Virgin of Virgins; it was both agreeable to the servants of God and also, as suited the times, invincible to enemies', Remigius was responsible for establishing the cathedral chapter. Interestingly for a monk, he chose to create a secular chapter on the model of a Saxon minster. The dean and chapter, which included many Frenchmen, were to govern the cathedral on his behalf and serve the surrounding area. Remigius appears to have set the pattern for the changes that took place in other dioceses, and his chapter forms the basis of the cathedral governance of today. A further legacy was the founding of a library.

His vast diocese contained some of the wealthiest abbeys in England, and he dealt with them with skill and tact while all the time emphasizing the episcopal rights against monastic posturing. He played a particular part in re-establishing the abbey at Stow, outside Lincoln, moving monks from Eynsham, near Oxford.

As well as carrying out his ecclesiastical duties, Remigius played an important role in consolidating Norman rule in England and in attending William I at court. He was deeply involved in the discussions at Gloucester in 1085 that led to the Domesday survey, serving himself as a commissioner for Worcester. Little is known of his personal life, but he appears to have been a man of great energy, willpower, practical skills and persuasiveness. He displayed loyalty to both William I and William II, to Archbishop Lanfranc and to his adopted church. His great legacy was the reform of his enormous diocese but the most tangible was the creation of the cathedral, and within the fabric we see today there is a tantalizing glimpse of how it might have appeared.

The West Front at Christmas.

Detail of carvings on the west door surround.

Still surviving above the north and south doors are open slots, providing the means perhaps to protect the entrances from above or to offer scope for use on ceremonial occasions. In the buttress-like walls flanking the entrances small windows lighting tiny chambers offer excellent views of the doorways. This building may have included accommodation for the bishop on the upper levels. This idea might explain the passages and spaces within the massive walls, a vaulted area at the north, thought to have been a garderobe, and the handsome spiral staircase at the southwest, starting above the ground level but surely grander than was needed simply for access to roofs. Two small windows above the southern stretch of the Romanesque frieze still light the surviving part of this stair. No trace of the halls where the bishop could have fulfilled his baronial duties or of domestic chambers survive, the spaces they might have occupied now subsumed into the main body of the cathedral. There is continuing debate as to how this structure related to the ecclesiastical building behind. Was it a freestanding tower with the body of the church a little to the east, the latter possibly the Anglo-Saxon

West Front detail.

church on the site when Remigius began to build or was it an integral part of an 11th-century cathedral?

The cathedral was caught in the civil war between Stephen and Matilda in 1141. King Stephen was recorded to have made 'a castle of the church of the blessed mother of God in Lincoln'. After Stephen's defeat the city was sacked, and the cathedral may have been burned, although the Peterborough Chronicle dates the 1141 fire to later in the year. There is surviving evidence within the West Front fabric of at least two fires in the early years of its existence. It fell to Bishop Alexander, nephew of the powerful Bishop Roger of Salibury, to restore the cathedral after the infamous siege and fire. The chronicler Henry of Huntingdon wrote of Alexander's work that he 'so remodelled with subtle workmanship his church, which had been damaged by burning, that it appeared more beautiful than in its original state, and would not yield to the fabric of any other building in England'. Alexander was well travelled, and his up-to-date enrichment of the cathedral bears this out. It is possible that he united Remigius' building with a newly built vaulted nave, and if this is so it was in the forefront of Anglo-Norman architecture in England.

The surviving work on the West Front demonstrates his knowledge of contemporary 12th-century work in France and Italy. He commissioned the elaborately decorated doorways we see today, which are thought to have been constructed *c.*1145–55. The carved columns, mainly replaced in the 18th and 19th centuries, bear comparison with the west doors at St Denis in Paris, adapted here to incorporate Anglo-Norman features, such as dragon stops and beak-head mouldings alongside continental colonnettes and dog-tooth detail. There is some evidence that the central doorway had attached column figures like those at St Denis or the only surviving in situ examples in England, at Rochester Cathedral. Although stylistically alike, the three doorways display a great richness and variety of carving. The Corinthian-type capitals can be compared to contemporary work in Normandy, particularly to capitals at St Etienne, Caen. Whether or not the figure columns ever existed, the overwhelming effect of the decorative work to the three doorways was of a highly complex fusion of nature and geometry into an elaborate pattern.

The small niches set into the buttresses on either side of the central door probably date to this period too. The southern one has a 12th-century figure, possibly intended to represent Remigius. Also of the 12th century is the blind, intersecting, round-arched arcading above the side portals. Small openings appear within this arcade, lighting the mural passage of the earlier building. The two western towers supported partially on the walls of Remigius' building and set back from the West Front were built in 1160–80, although they were most likely planned before Alexander's death in 1148. These display tiers of arcading composed with a variety of ingenious arched patterns, unique to each tower. Gables were introduced to the north and south elevations to conceal the awkward gap between each tower and the outer walls of the cathedral. These are decorated with elaborate diapering and sit above more rows of round-arched, blind arcading.

Alexander's most dramatic contribution was the commissioning of the frieze above the west doors. It was carved into a run of panels that were part of Remigius' West Front. The panels may previously have had a painted or bronze lettered inscription on them, a feature associated with Roman triumphal arches. Parts of the frieze sequence have been lost with the insertion of Gothic windows and the gallery of kings, but enough remains to give a clear impression of the impact of this sculptural narrative (see pp. 38–9). All this decoration reflects Bishop Alexander's up-to-date knowledge and his taste for luxury and display. An indication of the appearance of Alexander's nave can be detected in the central narthex or vestibule where blocked round arches to the ➤ p.40

THE ROMANESQUE FRIEZE

The carved stone frieze on the West Front is one of the great treasures of Romanesque sculpture in Britain. Its introduction by Bishop Alexander demonstrates his love of display and his knowledge of artistic developments on the Continent, particularly in Italy. In Rome he would have seen the narrative friezes on Roman triumphal arches, and his route to the papal city would have taken him by the newly completed cathedral at Modena, almost certainly inspired by Roman models, with Wiligelmo's narrative frieze. The iconographic similarities between this frieze and the Genesis scenes in the Lincoln frieze are strong, but at Lincoln the cycle is expanded to include New Testament images also found in mid-12th century sculptural decoration in western France. The Old and New Testament subjects of the frieze would have been familiar to the medieval viewer. They would act as a transition between the secular and the spiritual worlds, underlining the need for penitence but through the salvation stories emphasizing the love of God.

Right: original panel showing the torments of those guilty of the sin of lust.

Below: Original panels now on display in St James's Chapel.

These sculptural narratives acted as a visual depiction of biblical writings in the way stained glass would do later.

The southern panels are arranged to be read from the centre outwards. What was in the centre originally can now only be speculation, but there might have been a Christ in Majesty or even a Jesse Tree, an idea depicted in manuscripts that provided valuable sources for medieval craftsmen. To the south of the main door are scenes from the Old Testament. Lost panels most probably included images of the creation, and the story is picked up with the expulsion from Eden, followed by Adam and Cain tilling the land. Both these panels bear close similarities with the Modena frieze. It is also of interest that the acanthus-like plants growing between their feet are comparable to acanthus details on the north doorway, indicating that the carving of both the doorways and the frieze came from the same workshop.

The next double-decker panel shows the birth of Abel and Eve spinning. The narrative continues with God instructing Noah to build the ark and a depiction of the construction. At this point the sequence is interrupted by a framed panel showing Daniel in the lion's den, of which more later. The story of Noah continues with the dove returning to the ark, the animals and Noah and his family disembarking. This abridged story, however, is not so straightforward. Around the southern corner, now appearing in the Ringers' Chapel, are two further scenes, part of the ark on the waters

Far left: new carving of the Lust panel.

Left: Alan Micklethwaite carving one of the new panels.

(partially obscured by later vaulting) and the deluge with three figures, thought to be giants being overwhelmed by the flood waters. It appears that these were intended to be in the Noah sequence but that an earlier door through the panels, which opened on to a gallery, was not closed off, and a makeshift arrangement was made in which the two panels, neither completely finished, were shunted to the south wall. Sometime later the door was closed, and instead of using the existing carvings the Daniel panel was inserted, illustrating God's loving kindness and complementing the Noah sequence.

To the north of the main door the narrative is taken from the New Testament. Nothing remains of the panel that would have flanked the central entrance, and only a fragment of the panel on the pier between the central door and the north door survives. The remaining panels, except for one 18th-century pastiche, are all modern representations of the original scenes carved by John Roberts and Alan Micklethwaite, masons from the cathedral's own workshop. The originals, carefully conserved by the cathedral's conservators, have been mounted on the north wall of Remigius' church, now within St James's Chapel. Within the northern entrance recess on its south wall the story of Dives and Lazarus is told, the inner panel depicting Dives feasting with two friends and mocking Lazarus, who is being licked by dogs. The iconography of this scene has a Germanic source. The scene is followed by another double-decker panel with the death of Lazarus above Dives and his friends being tormented in hell, hell depicted by a gaping jaw. Lazarus is carried away by angels and, in the panel on the north of the recess, is received into Abraham's bosom. The cloth held by Abraham, filled with small figures representing the souls of the departed, including that of Lazarus, is symbolic of heaven. In the next panel six figures representing the elect in heaven, elegantly arranged in classically derived poses, are in conversation with each other. The final sequence begins with the harrowing of hell, with Christ standing on a prostrate devil and receiving souls from the mouth of hell. Here the mouth of hell is symbolized by a monster's head. The three final scenes portray the torments of those who have succumbed to lust, sodomy and greed. These graphic depictions would have left no doubt in the mind of the medieval viewer of the need for repentance.

The newly carved frieze in place on the West Front.

triforium and clerestory show the form of the upper levels of the 12th-century nave.

In 1185 the cathedral suffered serious damage in what was described as an earthquake. This provided an opportunity for the newly appointed bishop, Hugh of Avalon, to undertake major rebuilding. The West Front was not affected until the final phase of this work in the 1230s and 1240s, which took place after Hugh's death. The master mason Gilbert de Burgo, working with a mason called Alexander, who became master mason in 1240, probably played a part here. Given the wholesale reconstruction of the cathedral from the end of the 12th century it has to be a possibility that the intention was to demolish the west end and rebuild, making a new Gothic West Front the culmination of a major building campaign. It is difficult to account in any other way for the obvious kink where the 13th-century nave roof ridge meets the remains of the 12th-century cathedral at the west end. For reasons we do not know, though they were perhaps financial, this demolition did not happen. Instead, once again the West Front was dramatically altered.

North and south chapels were added at the west end of the cathedral, possibly to disguise the junction between the new nave and the old West Front, and perhaps inspired by a similar arrangement at Bury St Edmunds. Their presence provided an opportunity to alter the appearance of the West Front radically and integrate the existing elevation into a great screen, comparable to the recently completed work at Wells, where a full scheme of sculpture was created to fill the niches. The result was that the 11th- and 12th-century work was framed with masonry, decorated with tiers of blind arcading in Gothic Decorated style, providing continuity with the 12th-century arcading. The taller upper tier incorporates gabled canopies that would appear to have been intended for sculpture. The only sculptural figures provided, however, appear in the central gable, set under canopies like the empty ones and bearing a marked similarity to the near contemporary figures on the façade of Exeter Cathedral. Below these are two further figures, a king and a queen in similar vein. It is possible that Bishop Grosseteste, during whose bishopric this work was undertaken, may have deliberately favoured the extension of the existing idea of the façade, representing precision and restraint over the extravagance of figure sculpture.

The 13th-century repetitive carved arcading of the main front flows round the polygonal angle turrets. These anchor the façade to the ground and have crowning pinnacles with apex statues: St Hugh, who provided the vision for the 13th-century cathedral, and recarved in the 1920s, is on the southwest, and the swineherd of Stow, replaced in 1743, is on the northwest. The swineherd was a poor man who gave all within his means to the building of the cathedral and whose generosity brought him a place in its history.

It is interesting that this campaign developed motifs from the 12th-century decoration in the side gables. For instance, the diaper work there may have inspired the lattice detail in the upper part of the redesigned central bay and the big west gable. This lattice design, which became the leitmotif of the mid-13th-century designer, can be seen again in various parts of the cathedral but most prominently in the central tower, rebuilt *c.*1240 after the devastating collapse.

Grosseteste's ideas of light, elaborated in *De luce* (*On Light*), may be reflected in the importance of windows inserted into the West Front at this time. The great Norman central arched recess was made yet higher to balance it with the screen, given a Gothic arch and an intersecting arched Gothic window (replaced with Perpendicular tracery in the 14th century). In the course of this work all evidence of the 12th-century arrangement was lost. Above the Gothic window is a circular one with five cusps and plenty of foliage carving. Stained glass inserted into this window in 1858 depicts Bishop Remigius. It was commissioned by Charles Tennyson D'Eyncourt, uncle of Alfred, Lord Tennyson. Charles believed that he was descended from a kinsman of Remigius. Two circular windows were introduced above the new doors in the north and south screen extensions.

The middle and latter 14th century brought more changes to the west end as a result of the generous benefaction of the treasurer, John de Welbourne (Welburne). Once again it has been suggested that the object was to obliterate the Romanesque work. Within the outer narthexes this was effectively achieved by the introduction of lierne vaulting, blind traceried decoration and exotic blind arcading, almost

Moorish in its curvilinear form and elaboration. On the exterior much Romanesque work survived. Welbourne funded the introduction of the gallery of kings, an insertion that showed no respect for the mid-12th-century carving surrounding the central door: it cut off the top of the 12th-century mouldings. There is no obvious reason for this wilful damage because the gallery does not appear to align with anything else on the front elevation. The idea of a canopied gallery of kings was not new. Lichfield Cathedral frontage contains a full compliment of figures in niches and a gallery of kings (the figures were replaced in 1876–84), although closer comparison can be drawn with the gallery of kings set in the image screen at Exeter and dating from 1330–40, where the seated positions of the kings are similar to the Lincoln figures. Who are they and why should they receive such a prominent position? It seems likely that they refer to earthly kings and Old Testament predecessors, the latter wearing cascading robes much like those at Exeter, and the earthly rulers with their legs either crossed or together. This arrangement may have come originally from Notre Dame in Paris. The position over the west door would enhance the authority of earthly rulers but send a message that they were subject to, as well as enforcers of, divine law. The Lincoln figures, sometimes referred to as playing card kings, partly because of their characterless replacement heads, all have close-fitting upper garments and cloaks, adopt rather conversational poses and sit under highly decorative canopies. The West Front is not the only place where kings feature: more can be found in the carved woodwork of the choir and in roof bosses.

The gallery of kings. Although assumed by Victorian restorers to be kings, and given kings' heads, on close examination it appears that one or two of the figures were originally queens.

Towards the end of the 14th century a new Perpendicular-style window was inserted above the kings, and similar windows were placed above the north and south doors, continuing the trend seen at Durham and Norwich, among other cathedrals. Between 1370 and 1400 the impact of the West Front was further enhanced by the raising of the west towers, continuing the Norman octagonal angle turrets for three further stages and crowning them with two tiers of elegant blind arcading and slender lead pinnacles. Tall paired bell-openings, modelled on the central tower, were created, and their ogee moulding rises to the delicate lacy tracery that forms the parapet. Needle-like, lead-covered spires completed the work on the towers. By 1400 the West Front was essentially as we see today, but in subsequent centuries much further work has gone on, often behind the scenes.

From the 18th century onwards most work on the west end has concentrated on its repair and conservation. The architect James Gibbs, asked to report on the condition of the fabric, concluded that the west towers appeared to be forcing the walls below outwards. To resolve the problem he suggested introducing strengthening at ground level by ➤ p.44

CEREMONY AND THE WEST FRONT

The great west door provides the formal entry to the cathedral for ceremonial occasions. One historic example is Henry VIII's visit in 1541. On 9 August an imposing entourage entered the city, where the mayor presented the sword and mace and joined the procession. 'At the entry of the minster the mayor and brethren drew apart, the bishop of Lincoln with the choir with the cross being in the body of the church. The king alighted at the west end of the minster, where a carpet and stools and cushions of cloth of gold, and crucifixes laid thereon for the king and queen. The king kneeled down, the bishop came forth wearing his mitre and gave the crucifix to the king and queen to kiss, and "censyd" them; and then the king and queen went into the church under the canopy of the sacrament and made their prayers while the choir sang *Te Deum*.'

Royal visitors and their Lincolnshire representative, the lord lieutenant, are still greeted at the west door, and the mayor, when attending formal services, comes with Richard II's sword, probably that used in 1541, and the mace. The west door plays an important part in the enthronement of bishops. A new bishop has to knock on the door to ask admission from the dean and chapter.

It is also a place for liturgical ceremonies. The open slits over the west door may have been used in medieval times for hanging banners on religious feasts. Today on Palm Sunday the congregation line the path to the west door and throw branches of greenery for the choir and clergy to walk over, re-enacting the palms thrown before Jesus on his entry to Jerusalem.

The Duke and Duchess of York leaving the Service of Thanksgiving for the completion of special repairs in 1932.

Special souvenir programme for the royal visit in 1932, by kind permission of Mr Alan Goulding.

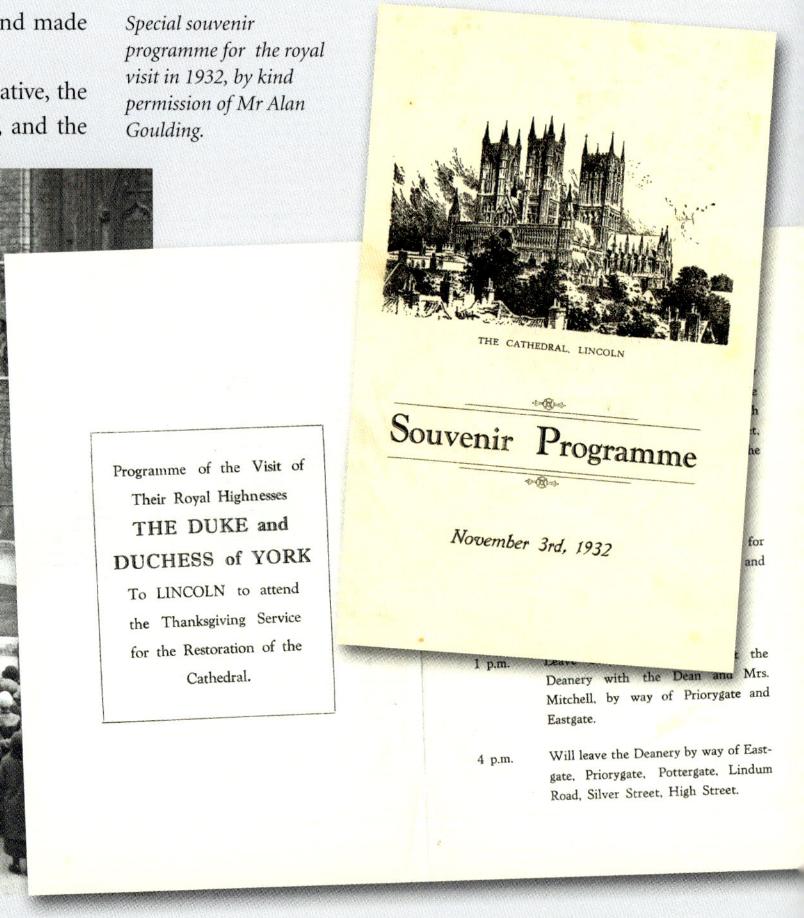

THE CATHEDRAL, LINCOLN

Souvenir Programme

November 3rd, 1932

Programme of the Visit of Their Royal Highnesses THE DUKE and DUCHESS of YORK To LINCOLN to attend the Thanksgiving Service for the Restoration of the Cathedral.

1 p.m. ... the Deanery with the Dean and Mrs. Mitchell, by way of Priorygate and Eastgate.

4 p.m. Will leave the Deanery by way of East-gate, Priorygate, Pottergate, Lindum Road, Silver Street, High Street.

Opposite: exeunt procession through the west door after the Battle of Britain commemoration service.

BRANCH
ASSOCIATION
THE ROYAL AIR FORCE

The Mystery Plays are performed every five years. Here, the stage was set at the West Front.

constructing screen walls, using stone from the old bishop's palace, across the width of the westernmost nave and aisles bays, with further walls tying back to the West Front, thus forming three vestibules or narthexes. Gibbs, known for his use of classical detailing, suggested a classical design, with round-headed arches and oculi above. The architect John James, called in for a second opinion, agreed with the principle of the strengthening but thought that the detailing should be Gothic. The Gibbs proposal prevailed, and the work, which is easily recognizable today, was carried out between 1726 and 1730. Both architects also suggested that the lead-covered western spires should be removed because of their great weight. Local outrage prevented this being done until 1807.

The architect to undertake the most important work on the cathedral in the 18th century was James Essex. The consulting architect at Lincoln for 23 years, Essex had a deep understanding of medieval construction techniques, which he combined with a concern for economy and practicality. He also made important contributions to work at Ely Cathedral and King's College Chapel, Cambridge. Like Gibbs, he was concerned for the structural stability of the West Front, but, unlike Gibbs, he carried out work in keeping with the Gothic style, in particular replacing the wall Gibbs had built across the nave with a two-centred arch flanked by blind lancets in sympathy with the surrounding 13th-century work. He also filled some of the cavities within the thick west wall.

The West Front had suffered considerable loss of detail, and Essex was responsible in the 1770s for replacing shafts around the doors, repairing heads of arches and dog-tooth detail and restoring the two figures of bishops. His work did not necessarily replace like-for-like, his philosophy being that 'since medieval architecture suffered from a "superfluity" of ornament, it will often be found that when one is defaced another may be taken away to preserve the symmetry, without spoiling the appearance of the work' and that it was 'not necessary to restore every broken ornament, which will waste much time and expense in beautifying the church. If the proportions are good the ornament will not be missed.' It is possible that one of the frieze panels depicting the torment of the damned was also replaced at this time. The programme of repair work begun by Essex continued well after his death in 1784.

In the middle of the 19th century the architect J.C. Buckler undertook cleaning work on the West Front and started a furious row with Sir G.G. Scott about the ethics of severe cleaning and the replacement of heads. On the West Front, where Essex had replaced carved colonnettes with plain ones, Buckler reinstated carved ones, using existing evidence for their form, and he argued that the chevron and beak-head mouldings surviving in the portals had to be replaced as 'a severe but necessary measure'.

J.L. Pearson succeeded Buckler as consulting architect, and he continued to have concerns about the west towers – the southwest one appeared to lean more and had suffered from the vibration of the bells. He took a second opinion from the engineer William Barlow, best known for his design of the St Pancras train shed. The proposals were agreed, and additional reinforcement was made to the southwest tower and a self-supporting concrete bell frame was inserted. In 1892–3 the northwest tower was repaired. The ground in front of the West Front was lowered in 1882–3, exposing the 11th-century plinth and resulting in a sunken semicircular grassed space separating the cathedral from the roadway.

The west towers continued to be a cause for concern in the early 20th century. The architect Sir Charles Nicholson and the engineer Sir Francis Fox forced quantities of concrete into the west wall during the 1920s and early 1930s to consolidate the structure. The use of an untried material was not questioned at the time, but it is becoming an issue for the architect today.

The biggest intervention on the West Front in the 20th century was the decision to remove the northern run of the Romanesque frieze panels to safe keeping within the cathedral. They are now expertly conserved by the cathedral's conservation team and suspended on the original Romanesque north wall of Remigius' building. This wall is now the south wall of St James's Chapel. Here they are protected from the elements and carefully monitored, while explanatory panels aid an appreciation of these important carvings. The process leading up to the decision to remove the panels was extremely protracted, involving national experts, a symposium resulting in an important publication, *Romanesque Lincoln: The Sculpture of the Cathedral*, as well as lengthy debates on cleaning and conservation techniques – not an approach that would have been understood in the 18th or 19th century.

Detailed survey found that the sculptures had suffered much more than the accumulation of dirt. They were, in fact, delaminating from the wall surface. Ultimately, a new set of panels was carved by the sculptors John Roberts and Alan Micklethwaite, in discussion with Professor George Zarnecki. The panels were unveiled in 2001 with considerable trepidation, some fearful that the explicit views of torment and hell, for so long partially obscured by grime, might cause outrage. Fortunately, this did not happen. The south run of the frieze remains to be cleaned, and not until this work is undertaken will it be known if these panels are also too fragile to be retained in situ. It is a debate that can have no absolutely right answer and one the cathedral chapter, Fabric Advisory Committee, English Heritage and the Cathedrals' Fabric Commission for England have to struggle with when funds are available to undertake the sensitive cleaning.

Meanwhile, the masons have continued repair work, an excellent example of which can be seen in the southern Romanesque niche, where the capitals of the attached columns have been recarved, and a monkey cheekily peeks down at anyone making a careful inspection. Today's craftsmen and women still work within the medieval tradition, leaving their own individual contributions for future generations to puzzle over and enjoy.

The congregation spills out of the west door after midnight mass on Christmas Eve.

THE NAVE

BY MARY LUCAS

Reconstruction of the original nave by David Vale.

From medieval times the nave of a church was linked to the ark of Noah, the ship in which mankind was saved from the great flood, and so the nave (from Latin *navis*, meaning 'ship') with its vaulting like an upturned boat, symbolizes a place of refuge and salvation, in contrast to the outside world. Noah's story was considered sufficiently important to feature prominently on the Norman frieze on the West Front.

The nave of the first cathedral here was a smaller, darker place, 10 bays long and vaulted by Bishop Alexander the Magnificent after it was damaged by fire in the mid-12th century. It was replaced with the present three-storey magnificent Gothic structure in the early 13th century, as part of the rebuild after the major collapse in 1185, said at the time to have been caused by an earthquake, which 'split it from top to bottom', implying total destruction. In fact, it was probably partial damage caused by structural failure (see pp.64–5). The rebuild started with the choir, then continued with the new nave, which was joined on to the surviving western block, which was widened to make a more splendid West Front, with chapels behind it to disguise the join.

Entered through the relatively confined space of the narthex, it is a breathtakingly huge, light-filled space. The development of the pointed arch allowed windows to be larger and spans longer, here with spans of over 26 feet, the piers slender, so that it appears as one huge space, which includes the aisles, an impression amplified by the soaring vault, 10 feet higher than that in the choir. It is a miracle of medieval structural engineering, a uniquely daring attempt to reach up to heaven, achieving beauty and power through apparent lightness of construction. It amazes us in the 21st century, who are used to seeing very large buildings; to the medieval pilgrim, unused to places larger than their parish church, it must have been even more astonishing.

The nave, looking east from Banks' view.

The elegant design of the tiercon vault, showing the carved bosses and painted decoration.

Right: detail of one of the roof bosses, with a painted memorial to Fricabon, one of the 13th-century donors.

The innovative tiercon vault springs from narrow shafts, seven ribs fanning out overhead in a pattern of arcs resembling palm leaves to a central ridge, each intersection furnished with three intricately carved bosses. This elegant design was so beautiful that it was copied at Ely and later at other cathedrals. The roof bosses that join the ribs are intricately and deeply carved. On either side of the ridge was further decoration: painted borders of scrollwork, still visible in three places, as are three of the original six names also painted next to the ribs: Braud, Paris and Fricabon – a unique sort of memorial to the generosity of these laypeople who contributed to the rebuilding of the nave eight centuries ago.

This great vault is supported on slender columns of limestone, embellished with clusters of English marble shafts. In the 1950s a former subdean, Canon Cook, used to startle visitors by announcing that the cathedral was 'the first prefabricated building in England'. He then explained that the dark marble columns were ordered to an exact specification from the quarry in the Isle of Purbeck in Dorset, carved, polished and shipped to Lincoln by sea and then up the River Witham. Evidence of this is the presence of identical columns in a church near the Lincolnshire port of Boston. These marble shafts are used in the nave piers and in much of the arcading throughout the cathedral.

The apparent symmetry of the nave masks subtle differences that enhance the richness and complexity of the whole ensemble. This was partly because the long timespan of the nave building meant that the masons changed, as did

The nave floor is usually kept clear of furniture but chairs are set out for special services and events. Here, the labels on the chairs indicate that they were set out for a graduation ceremony.

their individual style preferences. There is a riot of carving everywhere, on arcades, roof bosses and doorways.

A low stone bench running along the north and south walls below the blind arcades provided a resting place for the old and sick – hence the expression 'the weakest go to the wall'. There were no other seats, until recent times, when the nave was filled at first with heavy wooden chairs, like those in the Angel Choir, and later with the present blue plastic stacking ones, which are light and can be cleared away when the nave is not being used for large functions, so restoring the original appearance of spaciousness.

WINDOWS

As well as being a very large space, the nave is also full of light, from the two tiers of Gothic lancets, the upper ones in the clerestory in plain glass, the lower ones in brilliant colours, which illuminate its beauty and have a spiritual significance. In the 12th century the theological meaning was expounded by Abbot Suger of the newly built St Denis church in Paris, who explained that the light coming through the windows is the light of God, and when the stained glass windows depict biblical scenes the message is even more effective. This was especially true in a largely preliterate age when the windows presented visual lessons on morality. The theory was used by medieval glaziers, and the tradition continues. A sense of wonder is still palpable on a sunny day when the patchwork of coloured light makes an ethereal effect on the smooth stone of the floor and piers inside.

Most of the stained glass windows were deliberately smashed during the civil wars of the 17th century. The present

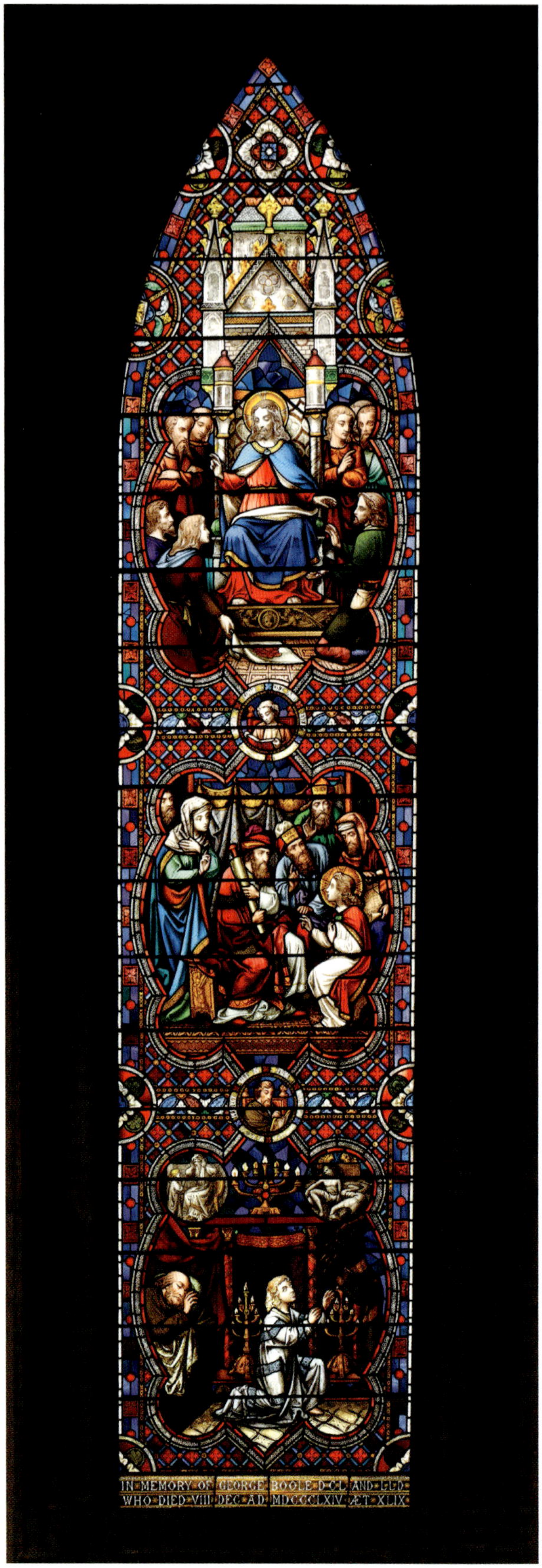

The Boole window on the north side of the nave.

nave windows demonstrate the Gothic Revival interest in reproducing medieval stained glass techniques and subjects. The colours are vivid, the biblical subject matter is clear, and they also show the dedicated skill of the best 19th-century stained glass designers, who filled the Gothic tracery with new designs. In 1858 the small cinquefoil window at the west end was reglazed, showing Remigius, the first bishop. The great west window followed in 1862, then all the aisle lancets, many by local amateurs, the Sutton brothers. The 10 on the north side contain New Testament subjects, the nine on the south side Old Testament ones. These windows commemorate local people and were paid for by their families, and one of the most eminent, though little known, is George Boole, a distinguished mathematician, whose theories of Boolean algebra led to computer design. He lived and worked in the Close and died in 1847. The window shows, appropriately, a teaching scene, including Jesus teaching.

FUNDING

Raising money for such a vast project as rebuilding the nave was a lengthy process and accounts in part for the timespan of several decades for its completion. The cost was met from various sources, including property rents from the cathedral's considerable holdings in the city and elsewhere and gifts from the 54 canons, many of whom were well paid. Bishop Hugh of Wells (1209–35) bequeathed all the felled timber from his large estates (much wood was needed for the great roof) and 100 marks to further the work. Gifts poured in, above all from the general public and clergy from all over the diocese.

To explain such generosity it is necessary to understand the doctrine of purgatory, by which all souls who were not condemned outright to go to hell or saintly enough to go directly to heaven, had to spend a certain period of acute suffering in this kind of halfway house between heaven and hell to expiate their sins. The time there could be shortened in two ways: by good works during life and by the prayers of others after death. So, for example, in exchange for a gift to the cathedral, Bishop Hugh of Avalon (1186–1200) granted remission of 80 days in purgatory (known as an indulgence) for contributions to the fabric fund. Donors could escape earlier and would be prayed for by the cathedral clergy, ensuring further remission. The works chantry was established as an official organ of prayer for the souls of dead benefactors. This fundraising was highly successful, but suffered a serious setback in 1217 when the cathedral was raided after the battle between the king and his barons, known as the battle of Lincoln Fair, and the precentor was robbed of 11,000 marks (more than £3 million in today's money), which had been collected for rebuilding the nave.

This belief in the urgent necessity of constant prayer to shorten time in purgatory in part shaped the building of the cathedral: to enable the maximum number of masses to be said or sung outside the regular daily services in the choir, chantries were founded. These were essentially funds bequeathed by testators to pay for special chaplains to say masses for their souls, daily, weekly and especially on the anniversary of their deaths for a specified number of years, sometimes 'for ever'. The rich often ordered these in groups of 30 masses, or 'trentals', to be said on consecutive days. In addition, they gave money for expensive vestments and plate to enhance the services and made gifts to the fabric fund. Chantry masses were celebrated at the 22 altars spread throughout the cathedral and in chapels especially built for the purpose. Among them are three grand episcopal chapels in the choir aisles and four in the nave. Here the dead were remembered, and the cathedral had an ongoing income.

THE WESTERN CHAPELS

Where the new nave met the surviving Norman west end, the façade was widened with Gothic extensions to the north and south, and behind it four chapels were built. The Morning Chapel, on the north side, is unusual in having a central marble column. It is divided off from the nave with a pierced stone screen. It housed four chantries, including that of Bishop Gynwell who was buried there. Further west is the Chapel of St James. It has an entrance door from the West Front, but no longer a dividing wall. Its southwest side is the wall of the original Norman cathedral. High in this wall the 'wynd', a chamber in the original western block that used as the cathedral's grim prison in medieval times. The chapel is currently used to house fragile panels removed

THE 'WYND': A CATHEDRAL PRISON

BY NICHOLAS BENNETT

This sketch, made in 1786 by the skilled artist Samuel Grimm, shows a group of men, including Sir Joseph Banks, exploring by means of a ladder a chamber in the northwest tower, which in earlier times was used as the common prison belonging to the chapter's jurisdiction in the close. The Chapter Acts show that 'le Wynde' was a prison under the chapter's jurisdiction, used to incarcerate clerks who had committed serious offences. Thus in November 1545 a poor clerk named Roger Rowth was committed to this prison for 24 hours for striking and grievously beating John Morryson, one of his fellow clerks. Again, in March 1546 one of the vicars choral, Thomas Parker, was sentenced to confinement in 'le Wynde' for being absent without leave for three or four weeks and repeated negligence in rising in time for matins.

A sunny spring afternoon illuminates the nave.

from the Romanesque frieze, which have been replaced by modern ones.

Opposite, on the south side, is the Chapel of St Giles. A chantry was founded there in the 13th century, and it was used as the Consistory Court from 1609 and is now the cathedral shop. Behind it is the Ringers' Chapel, where Bishop Hugh of Wells endowed his chantry.

One munificent benefactor, who founded his chantry in 1380, was John of Welbourne, cathedral treasurer from 1349 to 1380. He seemed to want to obliterate the remaining Norman style and replace it with 'modern' Gothic. His heightening of the western towers, remodelling of the great west window and insertion of the gallery of kings on the outside of the West Front were matched inside the nave by covering the west wall and ceiling with an elegant lierne vault, the walls covered with traceried blind arcading in the then latest Perpendicular style, so unifying the whole nave stylistically, except for the central west doorway, which still has its great round arch.

The large number of chantries, together with their 54 priests, was suppressed in 1547 as Protestants tried to eradicate the belief in purgatory by abolishing the means of lessening time there. Altars and shrines, with their accumulated treasures, were destroyed, and masses for the dead ceased, but the chapels remained, put to other uses.

THE NARTHEX

The nave structure remained much as it was built until 1725, when the architect James Gibbs made the first significant attempt to strengthen the west end, which was alarmingly weakened by the weight bearing down upon it. One obvious solution was to take down the lead-covered spires that crowned the western towers, but as soon as the work began angry citizens rioted, mistakenly imagining that the towers themselves were to be demolished, and halted the work. The spires were not removed until 1807. The second solution, which was adopted, was to strengthen the structure at ground level by the bold measure of building a

Detail of tomb of Bishop William Atwater (died 1521), one of many Lincoln monuments drawn for Sir William Dugdale in 1641 before their destruction in the Civil War. Dugdale's manuscript, now in the British Library, was formerly in the possession of the Earl of WInchilsea who loaned it to the Cathedral Library in 1922 for copying. The photographs were hand-coloured by Miss Helen Clements, daughter of a late Victorian Subdean [Lincoln Cathedral Library].

stout wall, in the currently fashionable classical style, right across the first bay, and another at right angles to it between the first piers of the nave and the west wall. The stone for this was to hand in the derelict bishop's palace across the close. It was used with Bishop Reynolds' permission, and his coat of arms was put up on the new wall in recognition of this.

These new walls created three narthexes, with small doors north and south into the nave aisles. This was structurally successful but visually unsatisfactory, because is destroyed the great vista from the west door right down the nave. This was rectified half a century later when James Essex, the consulting architect for the cathedral, was called in for further repairs. Among his many recommendations, he stated: 'In order to correct the disagreeable appearance of this wall, I was desirous of tracing the original state of this part of the church and if possible restoring it to the state which the builders intended.' He could not remove the wall, but he replaced the central section with a two-centred arch flanked by blind lancets and sensitively decorated all three openings in 13th-century style, restoring the visual harmony of the nave.

BURIALS IN THE NAVE

The nave is floored with large, smooth limestone slabs, but this surface dates only from the late 18th century. Before then there was evidence of over 200 burials, 90 of them spread throughout the nave, dating from the 13th to the 17th centuries. A few were county gentlemen or mayors of the city, but most were canons, treasurers and chancellors of the cathedral, with a group of four bishops near to the west end. In addition to names and dates on their tombstones, all had descriptions of those buried there and a plea to passers-by to pray for their souls. Many tombs had a brass plate with a 'portraiture' of the deceased.

Because prayers for the dead were particularly offensive to Puritan reformers and because brass was a particularly useful material for weapons, the Parliamentarians who captured the city in 1644 raided the cathedral. ➤ p.57

THE BELLS

Bells have played an important role in the life of the cathedral since at least the 12th century. The custom introduced into England by William the Conqueror of ringing the curfew every evening to warn people to put out their fires for the night (*couvre feu*) operated for only a few decades, but the ringing of the curfew on two bells in the northwest tower has continued to the present. There are 101 strokes, on one bell the number of the date – such as 11 – and on the other the balance of 101, in this instance 90. In the days before clocks were common, bells were also necessary to announce the times of the numerous services, and these two bells continue to do so.

The cathedral's oldest extant bells were recast in 1593 and 1601, respectively. These hang in the southwest tower as part of a peal of eight. When the vibration of their ringing was seen to be damaging the stability of the tower they had to cease. A new peal cast in 1913 again threatened the collapse of this tower, and once again they were silenced in 1918 until the 20th-century repairs made the tower safe. Four more bells were added as a memorial to the ringers killed in the First World War, and the last, 13th bell was added in 1948 to commemorate another ringer. It is on these bells that peals are currently rung by a team of volunteers every Sunday and on important festivals. They ring in the New Year, and on occasion attempts are made by the cathedral ringers or other visiting teams to complete long and intricate peals. They can also be heard during the weekly practices on Thursday evening, and 'joyful peals' can be arranged for cathedral weddings.

Right: the jack, still in the keeping of the master of the ringers.

Detail of the roof in the Ringers' Chapel, appropriately decorated with bells.

The Ringers' Chapel, below the ringing chamber, is part of the 13th-century widening of the West Front in the Gothic style. During the 16th century the ringers were gradually organized into a formal company, which set out their ordinances in 1612, giving them the distinction of being the oldest recorded company of ringers in the country. On the wall of this chapel is a list of the master ringers from 1614 to 1725, overpainted on an earlier list, which may be medieval, indicating a very long tradition.

Bellringing is thirsty work, a fact that has been recognized for centuries with the provision of ale, and sometimes bread, cheese and wine as well, for the ringers, in addition to a fee. In the 13th century there were three ringers, then four, rising to six in the 16th century. In addition to their normal duties, they were paid an average of sixpence each by testators who commonly asked for 'a peal in St Hugh's steeple at my burial'.

Before the demolition of the outer Exchequer Gate to the west of the cathedral in the early 19th century the ringers would repair to the inn there to quench their thirst and later to the Black Boy, now the Castle Hill Club. They drank out of a pitch-lined leather jack holding 22 pints of ale, which a local brewer presented to them in 1782. It belongs to the dean and chapter and is still in the keeping of the master of the ringers. The ordinances of 1612 required the ringers to behave 'honestly, modestly, orderly and quietly', ale consumption notwithstanding.

There is also a huge bell called Great Tom. The original was probably one of two large bells presented in 1180. It was recast in 1305 and again in 1610 in a temporary furnace in Minster Yard just outside the cathedral, which must have been a spectacular event as it weighed 4½ tons. This bell was hung in the northwest tower, where it was tolled as a passing bell until 1802 when its swinging was seen to exacerbate the instability of the tower. Its last incarnation came in 1835, when the cracked bell was recast along with six lady bells to make the present 5½ ton giant. This was done at the Whitechapel foundry in London. Its week-long journey back to Lincoln on a carriage pulled by eight horses caused great excitement, and the citizens turned out in force to welcome it. The enormous effort of getting it up the hill to the cathedral and then the raising of it up into the central tower was enthusiastically reported and enjoyed by large rejoicing crowds.

From 1880, when two more quarter bells were added, the clock chimes have been heard as we hear them today. From 7 am until 10.45 pm (the ceasing of night ringing is a fairly recent concession to the peaceful slumbers of those who live nearby) Great Tom is now sounded with a hammer rather than being swung. This great bell is also solemnly sounded on ordination days and major Christian festivals and is tolled on the death of members of the royal family, cathedral canons and other notable people.

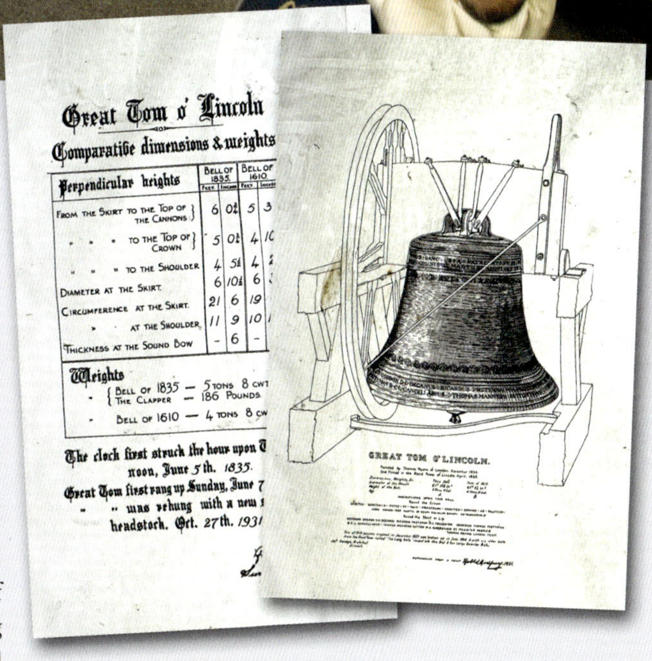

Great Tom o' Lincoln

Comparative dimensions & weights

Perpendicular heights	Bell of 1835 Feet	Inches	Bell of 1610 Feet	Inches
From the Skirt to the Top of the Cannons	6	0¼	5	3
" " " to the Top of Crown	5	0¼	4	1[illegible]
" " " to the Shoulder	4	5½	4	[illegible]
Diameter at the Skirt	6	10½	6	[illegible]
Circumference at the Skirt	21	6	19	
" at the Shoulder	11	9	10	[illegible]
Thickness at the Sound Bow	-	6	-	

Weights

Bell of 1835 — 5 tons 8 cwt
The Clapper — 186 Pounds
Bell of 1610 — 4 tons 8 cw[illegible]

The clock first struck the hour upon T[illegible] noon, June 5th. 1835.
Great Tom first rang up Sunday, June 7[illegible]
" " was rehung with a new [illegible] headstock. Oct. 27th. 1931

The bells are rung every Sunday and on important occasions by a team of volunteer ringers.

Left: Great Tom o' Lincoln.

Opposite: the nave filled with graduates and their families and friends.

The Romanesque font.

The contemporary diarist John Evelyn recorded that the soldiers hacked off most of the brasses on the gravestones and that 'these men went in with axes and hammers and shut themselves in till they had rent and torn off some barge loads of metal'. They also smashed stained glass window and defaced statues in a frenzy of desecration. Fortunately, such wholesale destruction had been foreseen as civil war loomed, and all the tombs had been meticulously drawn, their positions marked on a plan and their inscriptions recorded for posterity by Sir William Dugdale. The manuscript containing this information is still extant, and a copy of it lies in the cathedral library.

The floor must have been left uneven and damaged by the axe and hammer blows. Misguided 'repairs' of 1782 included repaving the nave with new, even stones, so that all traces of the burials there were lost in situ, although some of the gravestones were reset further east in the cathedral and the floors were left undisturbed in the surrounding chapels. This repaving also swept away two north-to-south lines of round markers, which had indicated the position of members of the clergy in processions.

THE ROMANESQUE FONT AND TOMB SLAB

Apart from its beautiful innovative structure, the nave contains several interesting artefacts dating from the 12th to the 21st centuries, including a spectacular font that dates from the 1140s.

Fonts have been traditionally placed at the western entrance of churches since the Middle Ages: because the west door is the physical entrance to the church, so baptism is the spiritual equivalent, the sacramental entry into the Church. The cathedral's black marble font has been used for baptisms there for over 850 years, providing a thread of Christian continuity since almost the beginning of its history. Its bowl, supported on stout round legs, is set in a square 'frame', which has a band of carving around it: animals and grotesque creatures, some benign, some fierce, probably representing evil defeated by the sacrament of baptism, and protective good in the guise of evangelists, the ox of St Luke and the lion of St Mark. This font was a costly import from Tournai in what is now Belgium, and it is one of only eight such Norman fonts surviving in England. It was most probably ordered by Bishop Alexander after he had seen a similar one in Winchester Cathedral, which he visited in 1141.

Another impressive import from the same workshop in Tournai is the black marble tomb slab, further east on the north side of the nave, which was also most probably ordered by Bishop Alexander. These are even rarer memorials, and only five are extant in this country.

It was customary to commission a burial monument well before death, partly to ensure that nobody could alter the design or skimp on the workmanship and partly to make a suitably grand memorial to the bishop's standing and perpetuate his memory and prayers for his soul. Alexander was very grand indeed, as his spectacular embellishment of the West Front still shows, and he wanted a grandiose memorial that would rival those of his fellow bishops, his uncle Roger of Salisbury and his cousin, Nigel of Ely, who also had similar Tournai marble tomb slabs. He chose a daringly presumptuous design – a Jesse Tree, showing the ancestry of Christ, from Jesse to his own tomb.

The slab is broken in half across its width, damage that was probably caused by falling masonry or beams

Opposite: the candelabra made in the cathedral workshop, its candles alight during the Christmas Eve service.

Midday prayers being led by a duty chaplain from the nave pulpit.

Right: portrait of Sir Joseph Banks by Sir Joshua Reynolds.

in the collapse of 1185. It was relegated to the cloister but was re-sited to the nave in 1872 and set on a plinth with an inscription mistakenly attributing it to Remigius, the first bishop, who died in 1092. It is now acknowledged that it belongs stylistically to the 12th century, and all the evidence points to Alexander as its patron. For all his grandiose building, in the cathedral and in his castles, Alexander was not known as 'the Magnificent' for what he built but for his munificent gifts to the pope when he went to Rome. His showmanship and ambition are hardly commendable Christian attributes, but these two Tournai pieces that he commissioned are significant enduring symbols of birth and death, splendid in their bold concepts, and a fine contrast to the pale limestone of their setting.

A contrasting memorial, also on the north side, is the 1857 tomb chest of Bishop Kaye, eight centuries later than that of his predecessor Alexander. The effigy is of finely worked, shining white Carrera marble. Kaye is actually buried in the churchyard at nearby Riseholme where he had the church built at his own expense, next to his bishop's palace (now an agricultural college, part of Lincoln University).

In 1915 another fine artefact was added to the nave. The huge 18th-century wooden pulpit was brought from the former English church in Rotterdam and given by A.C. Benson in memory of his father, E.W. Benson, who had been chancellor of the cathedral (1872–6), went on to become bishop of Truro and later became archbishop of Canterbury. It is a fitting memorial to a charismatic preacher who regularly attracted large crowds to the nave to hear his weekly sermons.

The fine craftsmanship of stone masons, carpenters, sculptors, glaziers, metal workers and painters evident in all this work in the nave continues to this day. One of the most recent memorials is the unusual copper sculpture mounted on wood of a plant, *Banksia*, discovered in Australia by the distinguished Lincolnshire botanist and natural historian Joseph Banks (1743–1820). Banks joined Captain Cook's voyage round the world in 1768 and was president of the Royal Society. He was a frequent visitor to the cathedral, which he liked to contemplate from the gallery high up above the great west door, known as Banks's view. An indication of

his passionate curiosity is the story that he was present at the opening of the tomb of Little Hugh in the north choir aisle. When the coffin revealed a child's skeleton in a thick liquid, Banks, in the interests of scientific research, dipped his finger into the liquid and tasted it.

Another wooden masterpiece is the series of carvings by William Fairbanks on the wall in the north aisle. They represent the Stations of the Cross in a modern, abstract style and are made from 139 different woods from all over the world.

The cathedral was originally illuminated by a myriad of candles, some as much as 12 feet tall. They were lit for every mass at every altar and often burned throughout the day. Today's electric lighting is distinctively modern: clusters of lamps with metal shades hang down on rods from steel brackets high on the aisle walls. They were designed by cathedral architect, Lawrence Bond. There is also an unusual candelabrum near the crossing. It was designed by the clerk of works, R.S. Godfrey, and made in the cathedral workshop out of pieces of copper tubing bent into a circle and surmounted by three delta bronze gilded magi. The lighting of its candles from below by a taper on a long pole just before the carol service on Christmas Eve in the darkened nave was always a dramatic moment. This simple candelabrum is a few yards further west of its ornate 17th-century brass counterpart in the choir. Both are beautiful in their own way and both demonstrate the high standard of craftsmanship evident in all the cathedral's artefacts.

Detail from one of the wooden carvings by William Fairbanks.

The Adam and Eve scene from the Mystery Plays, here performed in the nave [Courtesy of the Lincolnshire Echo*].*

Poster for the 1985 Mystery Plays.

EVENTS IN THE NAVE

Until the Reformation the choir was the unique preserve of the clergy, while the nave was the place of the laity and was always full of activity. It is an ideal venue for public spectacle, and there was plenty of this from earliest times. Apart from the numerous masses celebrated by the chantry priests at the various altars during the morning, there were many occasions for which the nave was a natural focus.

Every Sunday and on the numerous feast days all the clergy and their many assistants solemnly processed from the choir down the south side of the nave and back up the north side into the choir. The clergy were richly dressed in silk copes, the assistants bearing jewelled crosses, candles, censors and saintly relics in their gold caskets, and the precentor displayed the silver-bound book of gospels. They all walked in proper order, indicated by round stones set in the floor to mark their positions. There were also weekly sermons in the nave for the laity, with the inducement of indulgences for attendance.

Moral lessons were available in sermons and stained glass scriptural pictures, but another visual method of instruction with greater immediacy was liturgical drama, when great events of the Christian year were dramatized, with participants dressed in rich, often borrowed finery for the occasion. Religious and trade guilds of the city also brought annual pageants and plays to the nave. These retold biblical stories and also contained a humorous element in the role of unbiblical rogues and jesters to hold the attention of the audience. These mystery plays have been revived in Lincoln in recent decades and played in the cathedral by amateur actors, as they originally were. The archaic language is retained, emphasizing the continuity and power of such drama to teach and to move the audience, though there have been innovations, such as God being portrayed by a woman, but the essential redemptive message remains.

There was an annual Whitsun procession when representatives from each parish in the Lincolnshire part of the diocese came to offer their 'smoke farthings' to their mother church. This was a tax on each household with a fire. Such a large gathering often caused friction, as we know from the reproofs of various bishops about the disorder caused by rival groups beating each other with their parish banners. Large crowds also offered opportunities for other less salubrious activities: beggars pestered pilgrims, orphans were abandoned (to be transferred to the orphanage at St Catherine's priory south of the city), and there were even stalls selling souvenirs and vestments.

Another excitement witnessed in the nave by crowds of eager spectators was the punishment of wrongdoers in the humiliating public ceremony of penance. This was common in medieval churches but must have been particularly impressive in the cathedral. It was intended as a deterrent to other potential malefactors found guilty in the church court of such crimes as sacrilege, adultery, assault or witchcraft. Bareheaded and barefoot and wearing nothing but a white sheet and carrying a candle, the penitent had to join the solemn procession of clergy at the west end on three successive Sundays. He usually had to confess his crime 'for the edification of his hearers'. It must have been gratifying to the assembly when the penitent was of some status and normally richly dressed.

The most impressive gatherings of all occurred on royal visits, bishops' visitations and, above all, grand funerals. The detailed accounts of the funerals of two bishops tell not only of the solemn funeral in the choir but the preliminary procession, which was fervently followed by great crowds of citizens. St Hugh's funeral in 1200 reflected the popularity of this saintly bishop, who was, among other things, the tireless catalyst for the rebuilding of the cathedral. He died in London but was borne to Lincoln, where he desired to be buried. His body was met at the south gate and carried on foot through the city and up the hill to the cathedral with a vast crowd surrounding it, pressing as close as possible to touch the bier. Such was Hugh's renown that two kings and three archbishops attended the funeral.

A century later Oliver Sutton, another popular bishop, died at his episcopal palace at Nettleham, and again there was a huge gathering of people to escort him into the nave, with leading citizens carrying the coffin on their shoulders from the city's north gate. The funeral took place in the choir, but like all processions it passed through the nave first. This willingness to take part in such ceremonies shows a devotion to the mother Church as much as to the bishop.

The 16th-century Reformation was partly intended to purify the Church of disorder and abuses, but it also put paid to much of the awe-inspiring ceremony and pageantry – the drama, splendidly lit masses sung by magnificently robed clergy and pilgrimages to the cathedral's six shrines. The nave became a quieter place, although no longer the sole place for the laity, who were henceforth welcomed into the choir. One thread of continuity was royal visits, which, though occasional, continued to awe and delight the populace who came to witness the spectacle. Today even the service itself takes place in the nave with the laity taking a full part in it, sharing with the sovereign the joy and solemnity of, for instance, the recent presentation of Maundy Money by Elizabeth II.

Detail of nave vaulting.

THE CROSSING, TRANSEPTS AND SCREEN

BY MARY LUCAS

The crossing is the physical centre of the building, made in the shape of a cross, the principal symbol of Christianity. It separates the nave to the west from the choir to the east and has two magnificent large transepts to north and south. This part of St Hugh's rebuilt church was completed about 1210, before the nave, as building gradually moved westwards from the choir. It was built in two phases, the change in style visible inside the middle chapels on the east wall, where the wall arcading changes from double-blind arcading to single-layer arcading.

The lofty vault was decorated in a similar way to the nave. The ridge rib was again flanked with painted scrollwork. In the north transept the semicircles and leaved stalks were accurately overpainted in the 19th century, while that on the south side, revealed in 1962, is the original work and includes roundels, one containing a head of Christ and another the head of a bishop, possibly St Hugh. On the floor beneath were numerous tombstones, obliterated like those in the nave, during the repaving of 1783.

The cathedral with the original central spire, reconstruction by David Vale.

THE TOWER

The four massive piers of the crossing support the great central tower overhead. The Norman cathedral had no central tower nor is there any mention of it in the *Life* of St Hugh, so the tower that collapsed in 1237 or 1239 must have been a recent construction that was probably too heavy for its supporting piers in the crossing below. The chronicler Matthew Paris describes this collapse dramatically: Bishop Robert Grosseteste, a learned and strict bishop, was unpopular with the chapter as he insisted on 'interfering' in the cathedral's affairs. A sermon was being preached from the pulpitum by one of the indignant canons, who said: 'If we hold our peace the very stones will cry out.' Immediately, 'the stonework of the tower fell down and killed four people'. The mass of tumbling masonry also destroyed the choir screen and damaged adjacent areas in the transepts and the western bays of the choir.

The offending bishop 'set to work to rebuild it effectively', and it was finished before he died in 1253. Four massive supporting piers, new walls and other reinforcing work ensured its safety. This was a tremendous achievement at a time when much money was needed for other major building work in the nave and chapter house, and it represented a daring leap of faith. Then, in 1306, the bold decision was taken to raise the height of this tower and crown it with a tall wooden spire covered with lead. Bishop John Dalderby attracted funds for this by issuing an indulgence, and ➤ p.66

Opposite: looking up into the central tower from the crossing.

DISASTERS … AND DISASTERS AVERTED

The splendid medieval cathedral, standing apparently so foursquare and solid, suffered grave disasters over the centuries, causing serious damage, which was expensive to repair. Nevertheless, each successive renewal showed a remarkable resilience, optimism and strength of Christian faith on the part of the cathedral and the multitude of donors who made these costly repairs possible. They were, however, not content with mere replacement; they also aspired to ever greater complexity, size and beauty – a longer building, a higher tower, daring vaulting, huge windows, splendid carving everywhere and an eager embrace of new styles.

The first recorded major calamity was a fire that destroyed the original wooden roof and ceiling in either 1123 or 1141. The much heavier replacement stone vault lasted only a few decades before it, too, suffered partial collapse and major damage to the fabric in the 'earthquake' of 1185. This was probably an earth tremor, which exposed the structural weakness of over-ambitious vaulting on walls not intended to carry such a great weight.

The 'earthquake' of 1185 caused major damage and led to the rebuilding of the cathedral. Reconstruction by David Vale.

Detail from the 'timeline' window, created by the glaziers in 2009, showing major events in the cathedral's history.

Nothing daunted by the extensive damage, Bishop Hugh of Avalon started on the enormous task of rebuilding most of the cathedral in the new Gothic style, extending it eastwards and erecting a central tower. In 1237 or 1239 this latter structure crashed down into the crossing, destroying the choir screen and surrounding areas of the choir and transepts. Four massive new piers, walls and additional reinforcing ensured that its successor still survives, visible from miles away, a defiant statement of Christian aspiration. Until its soaring, lead-covered wooden spire blew down in 1548, the cathedral was the tallest building in Europe.

The disasters of the 16th and 17th centuries are mostly of a different order, due not to structural weakness but to man's religious and political obsessions, which led to the wanton destruction of many precious elements that had accumulated over time to embellish the cathedral. At the Reformation, when the worship of saints was deemed idolatrous, the gold and silver shrines of St Hugh and Bishop Dalderby were among the many precious treasures confiscated on Henry VIII's orders (they were removed 'to our jewel house in the Tower of London') along with much plate, vestments and jewels. Books, many of them exquisitely illuminated manuscripts, were burned and tombs were defaced in an effort to obliterate Catholic practice and beliefs.

A panel from one of the Victorian stained glass windows in the chapter house shows Cromwell's troops sacking the cathedral.

Further deliberate destruction took place during the civil wars, when in 1644 Cromwell's invading troops desecrated over 200 tombs by tearing off their brasses. In a frenzy of Puritan zeal they also removed the brass choir gates, knocked heads of sculptures and smashed stained glass, notably in the great east window and the Bishop's Eye. But the beauty of holiness is not so easily effaced. Fortunately, all these items had been recorded and carefully drawn when destruction threatened. The drawings survive, so we can at least appreciate them visually if not physically. Repairs were again undertaken and new features replaced the old, including the spectacular classical-style Wren library of 1674.

More recently, as the mechanics of structures came to be better understood and awareness of the significance of such a great building increased, structural disaster has been forestalled and successfully prevented. For instance, in 1724 a survey by the cathedral architect, James Gibbs, revealed that the weight of the western towers was dangerously distorting the walls below. His solution was to build a strengthening stone screen wall across the west end of the nave, forming the narthex, which temporarily averted collapse. Gibbs also recommended taking down the western spires to lessen the weight, but this was not done until 1807 as the citizens demonstrated against such a move.

In the 20th century drastic major innovative reinforcement saved a large part of the cathedral from perceived imminent collapse. The western towers were finally stabilized in the 1920s when grout was forced into the walls, and a concrete bell frame was inserted in the ringing chamber. The central tower was similarly stabilized. The east end of the building was rescued even more dramatically in the following decade by the casting of a continuous concrete beam, anchored into the east end from the eastern transepts, to counter the outward thrust.

The most recent potential disaster, the threatened collapse of the Dean's Eye, built in 1220, has been forestalled by the spectacular restoration of this magnificent rose window. The glass has been repaired and protected and the stone tracery replaced. Its rededication in 2006 was the culmination of an 18-year programme, a triumph of craftsmanship, modern technology and determination to keep faith with the aspirations of 800 years ago (see pp.68–9).

Meanwhile, the awareness of potential dangers to the fabric has been greatly increased by the publication of the 2001 Conservation Plan, which was commissioned by the dean and chapter and written by Dr Liv Gibbs. This meticulously details every element in the building, assesses its potential risks and proposes precautions against 'fire, wind, flood, structural collapse, explosions and earthquakes'.

Scaffolding inside the cathedral during the stabilization work in the 1920s.

Above: details of the central tower.

Right: the roof of the central tower, seen from the crossing.

under the mason, Richard of Stow, the work was finished in 1311, making the cathedral, at over 500 feet, the tallest building in Europe.

The sturdy tower remains, but its spire blew off in a storm in 1548, damaging the east transept. In the 18th century Joseph Banks was one of the enthusiasts supporting Dean Yorke's idea of rebuilding a stone spire on the central tower, but they were dissuaded by the argument of the architect, James Essex, that the weight would be too great. Instead, the traceried openwork parapet was added to the top of the tower. One suggestion for a millennium project in 2000 was another scheme to replace the spire, this time in light synthetic materials, but the enormous cost ruled out this scheme, and we have the majestic, awe-inspiring tower that crowns the cathedral, which surely needs no further embellishment.

Detail from the Bishop's Eye.

THE ROSE WINDOWS

The most striking features of the transepts are the two great rose windows, the Dean's Eye and the Bishop's Eye, high in the ends of the western transepts. They are described in *The Metrical Life of St Hugh* (*c.*1220) as the two eyes of the church, the Bishop's Eye looking south to invite the Holy Spirit, the Dean's looking north to ward off the influence of evil, so they must have been constructed in the first two decades of the 13th century, between Hugh's death and his canonization 20 years later.

The Dean's Eye sits high up above two rows of lancets, now a magnificent blaze of glory since its recent refurbishment (see pp.68–9). It is justly considered one of the finest in Europe, of few surviving from such an early period and outstanding both for its overall significance and its artistic quality. Its construction of slender stone tracery enclosing a huge mass of stained glass is recognized as a great feat of engineering. Like so much else in the cathedral the daring concept shows the faith and determination of the builders.

The central quatrefoil, which shows Christ in Majesty, is surrounded by four large roundels, each divided into four 'pictures', busy with biblical events. Between the roundels are trefoils containing graceful angels. The 16 outer roundels contain formalized figures of bishops, archbishops, angels and instruments of the Passion, with Christ as judge in the centre at the top. The odd one out in the pictures is in the left-hand bottom corner of the lower roundel, where a then contemporary event is introduced, that of St Hugh's funeral with the canopied coffin being carried into the cathedral. Before the restoration it was difficult to pick out any of these figures, but now they shine in their original brightness, linking present-day pilgrims and visitors to the time when this impressive and moving rose window was made. As the writer of *The Metrical Life of St Hugh* put it so long ago: 'The great windows of the transepts are like two heavenly bodies with their circular display … they outshine all the rest with their twofold light.'

Below this great window hangs a clock, a 'new' one given by the munificent treasurer, John of Welbourne (1349–81). The works have been renewed, but the clock canopy remains. Among other things, Welbourne also inserted the gallery of kings on the West Front, the choir stall canopies and the splendid new vault under the recently raised central tower. It is embellished with gilded bosses showing fabulous beasts, a hunting scene and a Green Man, rivalling the beauty of the choir screen below.

The original rose window in the southwest transept, known as the Bishop's Eye, was presumably similar to the Dean's Eye, but it was replaced in the 1330s with a striking design that was the fashion a century after its predecessor. Its delicate bar tracery forms a pattern of two adjacent leaves, quite unlike its counterpart opposite. It contains much of its original glazing, which echoes the subjects of the Dean's Eye, including a part of the original Judgement, as well as fragments reset from other windows in the cathedral, though much of the glass was destroyed by cannon fire in 1644. The refashioning may have been connected with the cult of Bishop Dalderby, buried there a decade earlier, whose candidacy for canonization was refused in 1328.

Below this window stands the bronze statue of Edward King (1885–1910). A popular bishop, he spent more time in Lincoln than his predecessors, when he moved back into the restored bishop's palace. He installed an altar in the nave and generally welcomed the citizens into the cathedral. His innovative Sunday evening ➤ p.71

Statue of Bishop King in the south transept.

The Dean's Eye restored.

THE RESTORATION OF THE DEAN'S EYE

The great rose window, high up in the northwest transept, has been known as the Dean's Eye since its installation in 1220. It is one of the earliest large rose windows in Europe, justly famous for its magnificent tracery, the fineness of its original stained glass and for the breathtaking audacity of its construction. It weighs 10 tons, and pressures over the centuries had twisted it four degrees out of vertical, causing weakening of the stonework and fracturing of the glass. A repair of the mid-19th century using iron cramps caused further damage and darkened the window.

Fortunately, modern technology, unavailable to earlier generations, has enabled the complete restoration and safeguarding of this magnificent rare treasure, which was seen in the 1980s to be in danger of collapse. Fortunately, too, the cathedral boasts a highly skilled workforce of specialist craftsmen to do the job.

First, all the medieval glass was removed, cleaned and conserved, revealing the detail and brilliant colours that had not been seen for centuries. Shattered glass has been repaired with invisible modern resin and adhesives and 70 per cent of the original is in situ. The restored glass is now protected on the outside by an extra layer, of isothermal glazing, ingeniously patterned to match the medieval glass inside.

The stonework was also found to be so badly cracked that it had to be totally replaced. The stone beds from the cathedral quarry were not deep enough, so stone was sourced from Cambrai in France, as it was the best match. The new tracery was carved to fit exactly in the distorted circle of the hole, using zinc templates made by a photo computer process that exactly replicated the medieval form.

A team of skilled craftsmen worked on the restoration of the window.

The completed tracery was exhibited in the transept before installation.

Grotesque of Dean Alec Knight winking.

The opportunity was taken by the stonemasons to add contemporary grotesques, as on the original. One of these is appropriately the sculptured face of Dean Alec Knight, winking and representing the 'Dean's Eye'. These beautiful carvings are barely visible from their great height, so an exhibition was held in early 2004 before their installation so that the public could see and appreciate them. Imaginatively billed as 'Once in a Thousand Years', this featured the huge jigsaw of the newly completed window tracery, laid out on the templates on the temporary concrete floor in the transept. Visitors could climb to the platform above to look down on the assembled stones, as well as seeing them close up on the ground.

The stones were then removed to be suitably reinforced, by the ingenious use of a stainless steel ring round the centrepiece, to avoid the pressure that had damaged the original, connected to the outer sections with covered steel rods, and steel anchors fixed into the wall, all these reinforcements disguised with a stone cover.

The medieval stone tracery was then removed, amid fear of collapse in this now vulnerable space, but elaborate precautions prevented this, and the huge hole was ready for the insertion of the restored window. The new tracery was allowed to 'settle' for a few months before the installation of the restored glass and its outer protective layer, with an airspace between the two.

The completion of this ambitious project in 2006 was celebrated by a great service in the cathedral in the presence of the Prince of Wales, who congratulated the team of dedicated craftsmen on their achievement. The restoration was necessarily costly. Half the money came from individual and corporate donations – as in medieval times when ordinary people generously responded to the need for funds to embellish this magnificent house of God. The result is a splendid blaze of light restored to its original glory, with its biblical messages now plainly visible in a fine stone framework in which the skill of our modern masons and glaziers have echoed the dedication and skill of the 13th-century craftsmen who worked for the same glorious effect nearly eight centuries ago.

Restoring one of the roundels.

Opposite: detail of carving on the central tower.

sermons filled the nave with eager listeners, and his memorial of 1913 was paid for by public subscription, an indication of the esteem and reverence in which he was held. These three bishops, commemorated in the transepts – Hugh, Dalderby and King – were all charismatic men who used their position to promulgate Christianity in a kindly and reassuring way, uplifting all who came into contact with them.

Bedesmen kneeling at the entrance to St Edward's Chapel.

THE CHAPELS IN THE WESTERN TRANSEPTS

As they step through a small carved wooden door into one of these six chapels, visitors exchange the awesome vastness of the nave and transepts for a small enclosed space with a distinct spiritual focus. The construction of these 13th-century chapels was a deliberate attempt by the medieval builders to create a beautiful, tranquil powerhouse of prayer, where a daily round of masses for the dead was said or sung before magnificently decorated altars by the incumbent priests, robed in rich vestments in chapels lit by many candles. After the abolition of chantries in 1547 the chapels gradually fell into disuse, until 20th-century efforts to revive them and give them a modern focus with a Lincolnshire emphasis.

South Side

There are three chapels on the east side of the south transept, the most northerly of which has an interesting history. It was part of St Hugh's rebuilt cathedral as a chantry for benefactors to the cathedral fabric, 'the works'. Masses were said there daily for their souls, and giving was encouraged by the issue of indulgences to donors, offering remission of time spent in purgatory – St Hugh proclaimed 80 days, and his successor 40 days – and for centuries gifts flowed in. In the cathedral library's 12th-century chapter Bible there is a list of benefactors who had a share in the 'spiritual good works' of the chantry. From 1321 the chaplains employed here were allocated a nearby house in the close, on the corner of Eastgate and Minster Yard, after the chancellor vacated it to move into the chancery to the east of the cathedral (now the deanery).

In the 14th century this chapel was rededicated at the behest of John of Gaunt to St Edward the Martyr, and an unusual three-tier stone screen was erected in front of it. It is intricately carved, has figures of kneeling bedesmen each side of the doorway and, above, a Latin inscription asking for prayers for the souls of donors. There is a royal coat of arms over the door. Much of this carving is a modern reconstruction to restore its original appearance as it had been severely damaged during the civil wars of the 17th century.

The middle chapel is dedicated to St John the Baptist. Three chantries were housed here from the 13th century, including those of Bishop Lexington and Bishop Dalderby, who was reburied in it after his shrine opposite was destroyed in 1540. It is currently dedicated to farmers and their guilds.

The third chapel, which is dedicated to St Anne, has a statue of the saint teaching her daughter, the Virgin, to read. It is now, appropriately, the Mothers' Union Chapel. It houses the tomb of George Tailbois (died 1538), one of the last great pre-Reformation benefactors of the cathedral. He was a member of an ancient Lincolnshire family that had come over with William the Conqueror.

North Side

The three chapels in the north transept are now known as the services chapels, since their refurbishment in the 20th century as memorial chapels to soldiers, sailors and airmen. The one nearest the crossing was originally dedicated to St Denys, the patron saint of France. It housed four chantries founded in the 13th century. After its refurbishment in 1914 it was rededicated to St George, the patron saint of England and of soldiers. Its deal screen is a copy of the 14th-century stone screen of St Edward's Chapel opposite in the south transept. This screen has brightly painted figures of soldiers, the warrior kings, Alfred and Henry V, and Edward, ➤ p.74

THE CATHEDRAL AND THE RAF IN LINCOLNSHIRE DURING THE SECOND WORLD WAR

Lincolnshire's large flat tracts of land and proximity to Germany are two factors that made it an ideal county for RAF air bases. There were 45 of these during the 1939–45 war, more than in any other county. They were built to a similar layout, often confusing the returning planes, whose pilots welcomed the distinctive landmark of the cathedral silhouette high on its hill, with red lights on the pinnacles of the great tower.

Most of the airmen were very young, conducting dangerous operations over Germany in cold, cramped planes. They faced constant danger and the loss of many comrades in arms with great courage and determination, as they flew out into the unknown in their hundreds every night in the mighty Lancaster bombers to weaken German defences and protect this country. As they returned, the sight of the cathedral represented for them beauty, tranquillity and permanence, which comforted and uplifted them.

They formed a force of about 80,000 in the county. Most were British, but there were other nationalities too. Many wrote of their wartime experiences in poems, letters and diaries, expressing exhilaration in the joy of flying and horror at the grimness of war and its high loss of life. One young Australian pilot, David Mattingley, kept a diary and detailed record of his time in Lincolnshire in the final year of the war, when bomber raids were at their height, and in 2007 his wife, Christobel, wrote a moving account of his exploits and feelings. The account reflects the experiences of many, but they are particularly well articulated here.

David Mattingley as a young pilot .

A serious, sensitive 21-year-old, who felt the heavy responsibility of his crew's safety, David Mattingley had a strong Christian faith and a fierce patriotism, appreciating the cathedral that he flew over so many times. He was ecstatic about his first visit in the summer of 1944, devoting a page in his diary to its beauty. That same winter he noticed its splendid shape as it rose above the snow that blanketed the county and mused: 'How wonderful the faith and vision of men so many centuries ago and their magnificent handiwork, still proclaiming salvation.'

In November 1944 he suffered serious multiple injuries from an attack by a German plane and was awarded the Distinguished Flying Cross for his courage and selflessness in bringing his plane back to safety, hiding the extent of his wounds from his crew. A month later, still hospitalized, he visited the cathedral on Boxing Day: 'Bathed in sunshine it seemed an epiphany, an allegory of light over darkness.' Listening to a performance of Handel's *Messiah* there reinforced his Christian faith, and 'he truly knew that his redeemer lived and whatever might happen, held him in His almighty love'. On 8 May 1945, VE (Victory in Europe) Day, while reflecting on the loss of so many comrades, he rejoiced that the war was over with the large crowd outside the cathedral, which was illuminated for the occasion by searchlights, as a joyful peal rang out over the city.

Returning to Lincoln years later with his wife and family, this heroic pilot proudly showed them the cathedral that had been so important to him during his flying career here. He became a life member of the Friends of the Cathedral, and the proceeds of his wife's book, *Battle Order 204*, go to the Friends, a fitting postscript to his appreciation of the cathedral.

A Battle of Britain commemoration service is held every year, usually on the second Sunday in September.

Detail of one of the stained glass windows in the Airmen's Chapel.

The Red Arrows fly past the cathedral.

The Polish memorial at Faldingworth.

MEMORIALS

The courage and sacrifice evoked in the book are honoured throughout Lincolnshire, where every World War Two air force station has a memorial to those who flew from Lincolnshire never to return. The death toll was horrifyingly high – nearly half of the men from the 110,000 bomber command, over half of whom flew from Lincolnshire or nearby airfields. One of the most recent memorials was erected on the former runway at RAF Faldingworth to commemorate the 657 Polish airmen stationed there who lost their lives in the conflict. It consists of three rough-hewn stone columns, two short and one tall, representing the three towers of the cathedral that was such a familiar landmark to these men.

It is fitting that the cathedral itself has a whole chapel devoted to the memory of these heroic airmen. St Michael's, the Airmen's Chapel, is perhaps the most poignant of the three services chapels as it commemorates lives lost within the memory of many visitors. Badges of two of the squadrons are fixed to the wall behind the altar, which is decked in Air Force colours and fine silver and blue cross and candlesticks. There is also specially woven carpet, pews with decorative donor sculptures and flags proudly displayed above.

A plaque records the number of the airmen from various countries who flew from Lincolnshire airfields and never returned, 25,611 in all. Most were British, but they also included 1,233 Canadians, 200 New Zealanders, 1,140 Australians, 90 Rhodesians as well as the 687 Poles also commemorated at Faldingworth. All their names are inscribed in three books of memory, one of which is always on display in a glass case. The others are housed in an ingeniously made wooden cabinet, which opens to reveal a wide, flat top to display the open book, which is frequently shown to visiting relatives.

The four fine stained glass windows in this chapel, made by Harry Stammers, are the only dated ones in the cathedral, 1953–66. They graphically evoke those whom they honour, from the New Zealand Air Force, Royal Rhodesian Air Force, Flying Training Command and Bomber Command, both those who died and those who survived. The clear glass background sets off the brilliant colours of the subjects: four huge archangels tower protectively over realistic figures of airmen in carefully detailed uniforms. Officers and men, even a dog handler, an aerial view of the cathedral, a collage of Lancaster bombers and the officers training college at RAF Cranwell are all precisely evoked. Forty years later, in 2006, the National Bomber Command memorial stone, commemorating the 55,000 who lost their lives all over the country, was dedicated in the presence of numerous veterans and friends, while the only Lancaster still flying made three passes over the cathedral, perpetuating the memory of the brave heroes, 'who gave their lives in defence of our liberty'.

Flags from the Commonwealth hang in St George's Chapel.

Details from the screen of St George's Chapel.

the Black Prince. All are carrying arms, and Edward's shield bears the cross of St George. The chapel honours the memory of men from the Lincolnshire Regiment (now part of the Royal Anglians) who lost their lives defending their country over 300 years. Regimental colours, the oldest dating from 1685, hang above the altar. All the fittings are in the regimental colours of blue and red. Memorials, gathered from various locations in the cathedral, have been assembled on one wall, and books of memory display the names of the fallen, with a new page turned each day. Pews, kneelers, altar rails and benches and commemorative windows complete this memorial. The stained glass windows were designed by Archibald Nicholson, brother of the cathedral architect, in 1920 in the Gothic style.

The central chapel housed the chantry of Bishop Oliver Sutton (1299) and is now dedicated to St Andrew as the Seamen's Chapel. It commemorates those Lincolnshire explorers and missionaries who undertook hazardous sea journeys to discover and govern new lands and who took Christianity to the other side of the world. Immediacy is given to their achievements over the centuries by the vivid images in the stained glass windows, which were designed by Christopher Webb and unveiled in 1953. They are dressed in contemporary costumes, emphasizing that they lived at various times. There is Captain John Smith, the intrepid adventurer who eventually became the first governor of the state of Virginia. His coat of arms behind the altar depicts three Saracens' heads, which he cut off in a challenge to save his life, thus enabling him to adventure to America. The first governor of Massachusetts, John Winthrop, is shown with his companions Lady Arbella Johnson (née Clinton, daughter of the earl of Lincoln) and her husband, in the ship named after her.

Exploration of the New World in the 18th century was greatly advanced by four other Lincolnshire men, and they are also depicted here. The eminent botanist Joseph Banks spent three years (1768–71) researching the flora of Australia and elsewhere during his voyage with Captain Cook, and he wrote a comprehensive book on it and was also president of the Royal Society. He took a keen interest in the affairs of the cathedral, being one of the objectors to the repaving of the nave and the loss of the ancient gravestones there. He followed the adventures of the contemporary explorers Matthew Flinders and George Bass, who explored Australia together in the 1790s. Bass was ship's surgeon on the voyage, and the Bass Strait was named after him. He disappeared on a voyage to New Zealand in 1803. He is also commemorated by the brass ship's bell from the *Tasman*, which hangs by the

Detail from one of the windows in the Seamen's Chapel, showing Sir John Franklin amid icebergs.

altar in the chapel. Flinders circumnavigated and surveyed much of Australia, drew the first map of it and in 1814 wrote a book, *A Voyage to Terra Australia* (southern land), which gave the country its name (it was formerly known as New Holland). A model of his ship, the appropriately named *Investigator*, hangs on the right of the altar.

Sir John Franklin (1786–1845) was an even more wide-ranging explorer, who also went to Australia and became the first governor of Tasmania. The window shows him as an Arctic explorer amid icebergs when later in his career he searched for a northern route to the Pacific and discovered the Northwest Passage. This journey cost him his life: he died trapped in the Arctic ice with his crew of 128. The two large stained glass figures are those of the sea-faring apostle Paul and the martyr bishop John Patteson, first bishop of Melanesia, who was clubbed to death by natives he had come to convert to Christianity in 1871.

This beautiful chapel with its 'history lesson' windows has its original wooden screen, doors and hinges of *c.*1370, acknowledged to be of exceptional quality, and is further embellished with ensigns hanging above. Woodwork and fabrics are evocatively decorated with waves, ropes, lanterns, the shell of Compostella, and a very modern touch is a gun cap from the frigate HMS *Lincoln*.

The most northerly chapel, dedicated to St Michael, also housed four 13th-century chantries and the tomb of Dean William Lexington. Its 20th-century restoration follows the pattern of St Andrew's next to it, in its modern windows, hanging flags and appropriate colours for its furnishings (see p.73).

All three services chapels are set in a background of delicately carved medieval stone. A small inscribed tombstone of 1290, set into the floor, is a reminder of the chapel as an ancient place of specific memorial. Apart from their commemorative function, all the chapels are regularly used for services on a rota basis, keeping alive a tradition of worship that is centuries old.

Matthew Flinders, by Helena G. de Courcy Jones, after an unknown artist.

Gun cap from HMS Lincoln.

The choir screen from the nave.

Right: the Green Man (top)peers through the carved foliage on the gateway to the north choir aisle and opposite to it a dragon (bottom).

THE CHOIR SCREEN

Until the Reformation the choir area was the exclusive preserve of the clergy and choir, separated from the congregation in the nave by a screen wall and locked gates across its west end. The splendid screen or pulpitum that preceded the fall of the central tower in 1237 or 1239 had six gilded piers and two wooden panels depicting the life of Christ, surmounted by a rood. The present magnificent stone replacement of the 1330s was built between the new massive piers that supported the new heightened tower of 1306. It was the location of the reading of the gospel during services in the Middle Ages. The cathedral organ has stood on top of the wide gallery above since 1702.

Intricate delicate carving in the Decorated style covers the whole surface of the screen on the nave side. The central gateway is an elaborate arch filled with 19th-century wrought iron gates, replacements of the brass ones removed during the 17th century. This arch is often covered with fresh flowers at weddings in the choir. The four buttressed niches on either side are covered on the flat surfaces with a pattern of flowers and acorns, and on the buttresses themselves, below richly

Grotesque, Norman Bonner, team leader of joinery (retired).

carved canopies, are figures of female saints. These figures were decapitated as idolatrous in 1644 and now have the heads of mitred bishops, after a well-meaning restorer of 1792 mistook their gender.

Above these figures is a quirky assembly of grotesques: devils, animals, dragons and, perhaps the most interesting, a portrait of a stonemason. He is not a handsome man, but his pointed nose, open mouth displaying broken teeth, neat hair and round cap add realism to the face, giving the impression that we are looking at a real person, an earnest craftsman whose features were carefully recorded by a skilled mason. His blue eyes are among the traces of the once bright paint that embellished the screen, making its impact even more astonishingly beautiful. A link with this 14th-century work is another craftsman's head, this time a living one – that of Norman Bonner – carved in the cathedral workshop in 2006 and now near the newly restored Dean's Eye, emphasizing the continuing tradition of this craft and the desire to immortalize one of its practitioners.

The fine decorated stone gateways to the choir isles at either side of the screen are slightly earlier. They, too, show a wealth of decoration – roses and dog-tooth, with stiff-leaf foliage representing vines, in three-dimensional carving over the arch. There are striking figures here also: the half-hidden head of a Green Man faces a dragon across the northern gateway. and on the south side men are seen slaying dragons, representing the triumph of good over evil. The whole ensemble is also a triumph of beautiful craftsmanship used in the service of God.

The screen was once brightly painted, and traces of the colours can still be seen.

Left: details of carving on the screen: a mason and a dog

SHRINES

Until the Reformation the cathedral had six shrines, which were popular with pilgrims. The difference between a chantry and a shrine was that a chantry was a means to help the pilgrim's soul out of purgatory and to pray for the souls of others already dead; a shrine had intercessory and miracle-working powers. Churches needed a shrine, which might be the tomb of a saint or, more often, a chest containing a relic, such as the real or supposed bones of a known saint. They brought in a considerable income from pilgrims, who came to ask the saint's intercession or hoped for a miracle to cure them or help in some other way.

During the episcopacy of Hugh of Avalon (1186–1200), an enthusiastic venerator of relics, Lincoln had no official shrine, and recognizing the need for one he 'stole' a relic for the cathedral. On a visit to the French abbey of Fécamp he was solemnly offered an arm bone of St Mary Magdalene to venerate. Hugh bit two pieces out of it, in what would seem a sacrilegious fashion for so holy a man, and brought them back to Lincoln, where they were placed on a newly consecrated altar, as was required by canon law.

Hugh also promoted the candidacy of Remigius for canonization. This was a lengthy procedure in which the sanctity of the candidate was examined along with a record of miracles during his life and after his death, using a biography to support the case. The pope then declared him a saint or refused the application. In fact, Remigius' candidacy was abandoned in favour of a much more immediate candidate, Hugh himself, a manifestly holy, compassionate, energetic and exemplary charismatic bishop. Miracles began during his life and multiplied after his death. He was the only Lincoln saint ever officially canonized, and in 1280 had two shrines at the east end of the cathedral, one for the body and another for the head.

Two other bishops who were revered locally as saints, Robert Grosseteste (d.1253) and John Dalderby (d.1320), were refused official canonization but had splendid large shrines, which were very popular.

The sixth shrine was that of Little Hugh, a Christian child who lived in the Jewish quarter of the city. His body was interred in the cathedral with great pomp after his murder, allegedly by the Jews, in 1255, at a time when Jews were becoming unpopular. Feeding on this false accusation, the persecution of the Jewish community in Lincoln is part of what we now consider a shameful history of prejudice. In recognition of this, a new plaque was displayed beside Little Hugh, written by the cathedral in conjunction with the Jewish community. It was dedicated in a most moving ceremony following an Evensong in October 2009 at which a rabbi sang the Jewish 'Kaddish for Mourners'.

Little Hugh's shrine attracted many pilgrims and donations, but never as many as those of the bishop saints. The story appealed to the popular imagination, and ballads were written in English and French, by Chaucer and others, telling the story of a boy lured to his death. Crucified and then thrown down a well to hide the crime, he continued to speak after his death and 'told' his mother where his body was to be found so that the crime was discovered.

All these shrines were elaborately built and decorated. They were also bejewelled, since pilgrims and testators offered gold rings or jewels to nail on to the shrine. In the case of St Hugh's shrine, such offerings were being made right up until the destruction of the shrine and removal of its treasures in 1540 on the orders of Henry VIII. All the shrines were either defaced or demolished at the Reformation, when saint worship was banned as idolatrous. The scale of their magnificence is indicated by the treasurer's recording that sapphires, gold images, pearls and crosses and 4,285 ounces of gold and 2,621 ounces of silver were removed from the shrines. So thorough was this purge that St Hugh's body shrine disappeared and the head shrine, dating from *c.*1350, is one of only three shrine bases surviving in England from this period. Only the reliquary containing the head was removed. Its importance to the cathedral was emphasized when a modern canopy was installed over it in 1986 to mark the 800th anniversary of St Hugh's enthronement in Lincoln.

Right: a pilgrim carved on an outside gable of the consistory court, now the shop.

Below: plaque recording the persecution of the Jews in Lincoln.

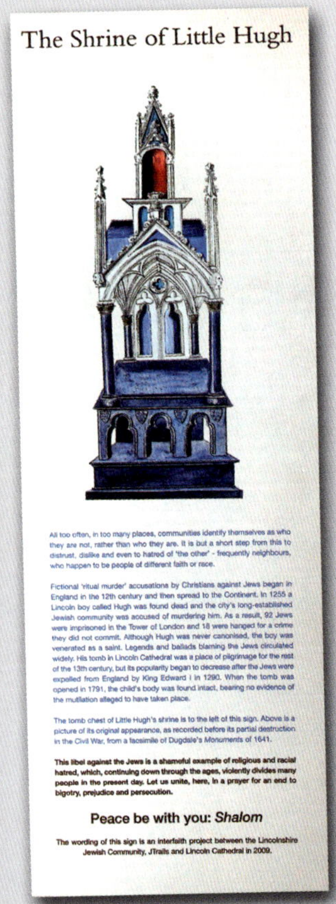
The Shrine of Little Hugh

All too often, in too many places, communities identify themselves as who they are not, rather than who they are. It is but a short step from this to distrust, dislike and even to hatred of 'the other' - frequently neighbours, who happen to be people of different faith or race.

Fictional 'ritual murder' accusations by Christians against Jews began in England in the 12th century and then spread to the Continent. In 1255 a Lincoln boy called Hugh was found dead and the city's long-established Jewish community was accused of murdering him. As a result, 92 Jews were imprisoned in the Tower of London and 18 were hanged for a crime they did not commit. Although Hugh was never canonised, the boy was venerated as a saint. Legends and ballads blaming the Jews circulated widely. His tomb in Lincoln Cathedral was a place of pilgrimage for the rest of the 13th century, but its popularity began to decrease after the Jews were expelled from England by King Edward I in 1290. When the tomb was opened in 1791, the child's body was found intact, bearing no evidence of the mutilation alleged to have taken place.

The tomb chest of Little Hugh's shrine is to the left of this sign. Above is a picture of its original appearance, as recorded before its partial destruction in the Civil War, from a facsimile of Dugdale's *Monuments* of 1641.

This libel against the Jews is a shameful example of religious and racial hatred, which, continuing down through the ages, violently divides many people in the present day. Let us unite, here, in a prayer for an end to bigotry, prejudice and persecution.

Peace be with you: *Shalom*

The wording of this sign is an interfaith project between the Lincolnshire Jewish Community, JTrails and Lincoln Cathedral in 2009.

Opposite: detail of carved boss in the central tower.

ST HUGH'S CHOIR AND THE ANGEL CHOIR

BY GAVIN KIRK

The main entrance to St Hugh's Choir is the pulpitum or choir screen. The original was damaged in the collapse of the great central tower in the early 13th century, which also caused some damage to the first bay of the choir. It was rebuilt in the Decorated Gothic style in the early 14th century, and decorated is certainly the word here: the pulpitum is almost covered by intricate carving, much of it forming a floral background but abounding with representations of humans, animals and mythical beasts. When we consider that in its original state the screen would have been richly painted we can appreciate something of its dramatic impact, and we can still see remnants of the coloured paint and gilding that once covered the cathedral. The red and the blue traces are significant: blue represented heaven, whereas red spoke of earth. These colours are most often seen on the clothes of statues and pictures of the Blessed Virgin Mary. Mary's bearing of Jesus, who was both divine and human, is seen as the meeting-place of earth and heaven, as, of course, is the cathedral, dedicated to her under the title of the Blessed Virgin Mary of Lincoln. During the Commonwealth in the 17th century many of the carvings were vandalized, but some of the heads have been restored.

The central arch of the choir screen decorated with lilies for Easter.

Through the pulpitum we may enter St Hugh's Choir, the 'church within a church' and the heart of the cathedral's life and mission, where choral worship is offered daily on weekdays and three times on Sundays. Apart from the westernmost bay, it is essentially as built under St Hugh in the early Gothic style. This style, incorporating pointed arches and lancet windows, was so named because it was seen as daring and revolutionary (like the marauding Goths). Indeed, it stands in marked contrast to the Galilee Chapel at Durham Cathedral, built at much the same time but still in the established Romanesque style. Whereas the Romanesque style, borrowed from the emperor's basilica, drew the eye to the end point of the building where the seat of power (the governor's chair, the bishop's throne) was, the Gothic style, with pointed arches and more delicate windows admitting more light, lifts the eye and the soul upwards, towards heaven.

The beautifully carved choir stalls date from the 14th century, but the matching bishop's throne (*cathedra*, hence cathedral) and the five stalls opposite were added later. The worship of God on earth is seen as participating in, and leading to, the eternal worship of the angels in heaven, and so there are many carvings of angels playing musical instruments. Some of the misericords are particularly fine. These are ledges on the underside of the stall seats on which it is possible to rest when the seat is raised – of particular comfort to tired canons during long periods of standing.

Opposite: a visiting choir rehearses the procession out of Evensong.

ROBERT GROSSETESTE

Robert Grosseteste's origins were humble, which may account for the lack of evidence regarding his early years. It is thought that he was born *c.*1170 in Suffolk and that his native language, like his surname, was Norman French. Links with Lincoln diocese can be traced back as far as the early years of St Hugh's time as bishop (1186–1200). He was a prodigious scholar, linguist and writer, and it is known that he taught the liberal arts, though whether at Paris, Hereford or Oxford is less clear; it is possible he was at all three. Many think that he was the first chancellor of Oxford University, which was founded in 1214, though the title was not employed at that stage.

As an academic he was learned in natural sciences, medicine, law, languages and theology. He studied Greek and Hebrew in order to understand the Bible better, translating several classical, philosophical and biblical works into Latin. Significant amounts of his treatises have survived on subjects as diverse as the metaphysics of light and the *Filioque* controversy over the text of the Nicene Creed. He welcomed the Franciscans to Oxford and was the first lector at the theological school they opened there in 1224. He seems to have been much influenced by the friars' life of poverty and preaching tours.

Chalice and paten of silver gilt, used by Robert Grosseteste and found in his tomb in 1782: now in the treasury.

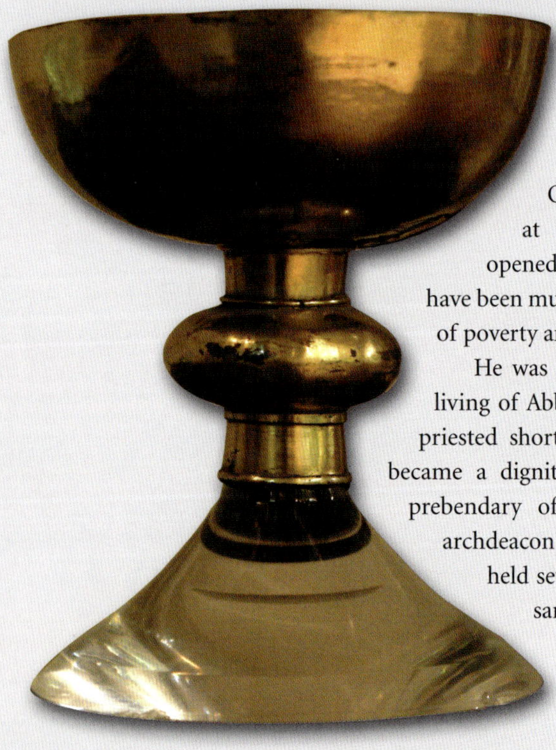

He was presented as a deacon to the living of Abbotsley in 1225 and doubtless priested shortly thereafter, for in 1229 he became a dignitary of Lincoln Cathedral as prebendary of Leicester St Margaret and archdeacon of Leicester. He seems to have held several ecclesiastical posts at the same time, a common practice in his day, but resigned all save his Lincoln canonry following an illness in 1231, stating that he could not in conscience retain those posts whose duties he could no longer fulfil.

He was elected bishop of Lincoln on 27 March 1235 as a compromise candidate, the canons of Lincoln being unable to agree on any other. From the outset he was determined to be a pastoral bishop, seeking to implement the reforms of the Fourth Lateran Council. He was especially concerned to provide able clergy to staff the parishes of his diocese, and, with two-thirds of these in the patronage of religious orders or other private patrons, he soon came into conflict with the monastic houses and, indeed, his own cathedral chapter, with whom he engaged in a six-year dispute over his rights of visitation. In his first tour of his diocese he deposed no fewer than seven abbots, and he fought tenaciously to prevent absentee clergy being appointed from abroad. He even opposed Pope Innocent IV when he tried to appoint a nephew to a Lincoln canonry.

He published numerous works on ecclesiastical discipline, the art of preaching, the hearing of confessions, biblical exegesis and moral theology, many of which were still in use 200 years after his death in 1253. Several unsuccessful attempts were made after his death to have him declared a saint.

Hoop from Grosseteste's crozier. Translated, the inscription reads: 'Through the shape of the staff learn the ideal of episcopacy'.

The choir stalls prepared for a service.

The 53 canons or prebendaries of Lincoln have their stalls (official seats) on the upper tier here. The tablet hanging in each stall bears the name of the prebend, which is either a place in the medieval diocese whose lands provided the income for the canon or the value of the stipend itself. Between them, the College of Canons recites the entire psalter daily, and the Latin opening words of each canon's daily psalms are also written on the tablet and shown to the canon during their installation ceremony.

The second tier of stalls was occupied by the senior vicars. The Latin word *vicar* means 'substitute', and the vicars were more junior clergy who were employed by the prebendaries to represent them at the services in order to free them for (lucrative) work elsewhere. The vicars were paid by a levy on the incomes of the non-residents, and they were accommodated in a college still known as Vicars' Court. The lowest tier was for the junior vicars, whose number included what we would now call choristers, singing men, servers and clerks.

Today most of the canons of Lincoln are parish priests or diocesan officers, but the senior ones are known as

Left: tablet in the stall used by the canon of Holy Cross.

residentiary – that is, they live in the close and work in and from the cathedral. In the Middle Ages there were five dignitaries, but over the years they have been reduced to four. They are the dean (who is the chairman of the chapter, the cathedral's governing body, and of the College of Canons), the precentor (who is responsible for all the services and music of the cathedral and for the plate in the treasury), the chancellor (who oversees the library and educational work) and the subdean (who is charged with the pastoral care of the congregation and is also master of the cathedral fabric). ➤ p.86

ST HUGH

Hugh was born in the village of Avalon in Dauphiné in 1135 to William, seigneur of Avalon and his wife Anna, who died when Hugh was only eight. William retired to the Augustinian priory of Villard-Benoit, followed by the 10-year-old Hugh. Hugh excelled in the monastery, being ordained deacon in 1154 and sent as prior to the nearby house at Saint-Maximin in 1159. He seems to have desired a more enclosed life than that of an Augustinian canon and transferred to become a Carthusian monk at the Grande Chartreuse near Grenoble. Although initially troubled by unmonastic thoughts and visions, Hugh rose swiftly within the Charterhouse and was appointed its procurator (bursar), developing a reputation for holiness and organizational ability in equal measure.

Far right: Seal of St Hugh, attached to a charter dated 1189–1193 [Lincoln Cathedral Library].

Medieval sculpture showing St Hugh with his swan, now in the cloister of New College, Oxford. This sculpture was restored in 2009 by Antonia Hockton who trained as a conservator at Lincoln Cathedral.

As part of his penance for the murder of Archbishop Thomas Becket in 1170, Henry II had been required to found three religious houses, one of which was England's first Charterhouse at Witham in Somerset. The first two superiors had proved ineffective, and Henry, having heard something of Hugh's reputation, sent a deputation to ask that Hugh be sent as prior. Hugh had to be required under monastic obedience to accede but did so and became the third prior of Witham in 1179. On taking over his new responsibilities, he found the monastery only partly built, seriously under-funded and Carthusian life compromised in several respects. An injection of royal cash and some controversial decisions by the prior saw matters improve on all fronts, and the king on his regular visits must have been impressed by developments at 'his' Charterhouse.

A synod at Eynsham in May 1186 had discussed various aspects of Church life, including the number of vacant bishoprics, a subject on which Hugh had already lobbied the king. The diocese of Lincoln had been vacant for over two years, and the canons were ordered to elect a new bishop: they chose the prior of Witham. Hugh had never even seen Lincolnshire or its cathedral, which lay in ruins following an earthquake in 1185. Ordained bishop in September 1186, he set off for Lincoln accompanied by one of the lay brothers from Witham. Although probably unable to speak English, he seems to have endeared himself to the people of his vast diocese by his regular visitations and his evident pastoral concern for them. His reputation for holiness might have preceded him, but his care for the poor, the young, those suffering from leprosy and mental illness, not to mention

Left: St Hugh's tame swan became his symbol. Detail from St Hugh's window.

his enthusiasm for burying the corpse of any pauper he happened upon, revealed more eloquently than words the priorities of Lincoln's new bishop.

Experience as procurator and prior must have proved invaluable as Hugh sought to administer the diocese, which in those days reached from the river Humber to the river Thames. He seems to have had a knack of spotting talented people, both administrators and scholars, whom he brought to Lincoln, turning his headquarters into an intellectual powerhouse and vehicle for reform.

Bishop Hugh was keen to improve the standards and lifestyle of his clergy, and equally determined to preserve the privileges and position of the church he served. Almost as soon as he was appointed to Lincoln he courted Henry II's anger by excommunicating his chief forester and refusing to install a royal favourite as a prebendary of his cathedral. Neither was he afraid to threaten hellfire and damnation when a king infringed the Church's rights or violated its precepts. In many ways he was as much a thorn in the royal side as Becket had been, and it may be that the archbishop's recent murder served to protect Hugh and enabled him to be the 'hammer' of the three kings whose reigns spanned the time he was bishop.

Although he appears to have been fearless in reproving and admonishing high and humble alike, it seems he was possessed of a charismatic personality and subtle wit, which more than once prevented a sensitive situation from escalating into a crisis. Moreover, the actions and lifestyles of the kings, Henry II, Richard I and John, gave cause for each to worry about their eternal reward, so continued good relations with a bishop as transparently holy as Hugh offered a measure of reassurance of divine favour.

Among the groups whose interests Hugh championed were the Jews. In an age that sought to isolate and demonize those who held heterodox religious beliefs, Hugh was unusual in offering the Jewish community protection and advocacy, ensuring that the atrocities that happened elsewhere did not occur in Lincoln.

Hugh's most concrete bequest is his work in rebuilding his cathedral. Only the westernmost bay of the original Romanesque building survived the earthquake in the year before his translation and he worked tirelessly to raise the funds and secure the personnel for the work of restoration and renewal. His own first-hand knowledge of church building in Grenoble and Witham and his choice of master mason Geoffrey de Noiers resulted in the erection of the first cathedral in England in the new Early English style. Hugh maintained a keen interest in the building work, reputedly assisting as a labourer whenever possible, and while he did not live to see the nave and transepts completed, he had rebuilt the choir, which today bears his name, and an apsidal east end.

Although bishop of Lincoln, Hugh never forgot his Carthusian vocation and continued to spend part of each summer in retreat with his former community at Witham. The rigours and privations of his monastic years, combined with his indefatigable service as diocesan bishop and royal counsellor had long caused eye strain and digestive trouble. A diplomatic visit to France in 1199 on behalf of the king exacerbated matters and the following year he fell seriously ill while attending a meeting in London, dying there on 16 November. His funeral was attended by two kings and many senior church figures. Almost as soon as he was buried in the cathedral the reports of miracles began, and only 20 years later he was proclaimed a saint.

Below: St Hugh helps rebuild the cathedral after the earthquake. Detail from St Hugh's window.

STALLS AND MISERICORDS

The notable stalls in St Hugh's Choir provide the seating for the Cathedral Foundation – that group of laypeople and clergy who maintain the life, worship and mission of Lincoln Cathedral. Completed towards the end of the 1370s by woodcarvers who are believed to have gone on to work at Chester Cathedral, they contain 53 stalls for the prebendaries or College of Canons. This group, which since the year 2000 has included lay canons as well as clergy, was originally maintained by the *praebendum* (income) derived from the property or endowment appearing on the top of the tablet. Some of these were quite substantial, and this led to the canonries being held, often in plurality with other positions, by absentee foreign churchmen. The precentorship is a case in point, being held in the 13th and 14th centuries by a number of foreign bishops who rarely, if ever, set foot in the cathedral but nevertheless enjoyed the revenues of the position, leaving a poorly paid junior priest to fulfil its obligations. One such dignitary, known as the 'Italian monkey', is represented on the poppy-head (the decorated trefoil end) of the precentor's stall. Here is portrayed a pair of monkeys churning butter (representing the rich emoluments of the position), a monkey stealing butter and, closest to the precentor himself, the same monkey being hanged for his crime. It seems that the person at whom the jibe was directed never in fact saw the insult, which rather supports the point the carvings none-too-subtly make.

Misericord showing burial of the monkey after hanging.

Detail of one of choir stalls, showing a frog disembowelling itself.

Assistant organist Ben Chewter playing the organ. The video screen above the organ enables the organist to see what is happening in the nave.

Set into the floor of the choir is a grey, bone-shaped stone inscribed with the Latin words *Cantate Hic* (sing here). This is the place where up to four of the medieval vicars stood to sing certain parts of the services. Before the Reformation the projection that forms a canopy over the pulpitum entrance was an ambo from which the lessons at mass were chanted. Now the lessons are proclaimed from the great brass eagle lectern, which was provided in 1667.

Towering above the pulpitum is the largest of the cathedral's four organs, the Father Willis. Installed by Henry Willis in 1898, it is the least altered example of his work in an English cathedral. It was last restored in 1998 and has been played in concert by some of the finest players internationally. It is known throughout the organ world for the quality of its workmanship. In the body of the choir is a small, modern chamber organ, used to accompany Tudor music, and there are also organs at the west end and the east end of the cathedral.

Far above, the irregular pattern of the roof ribs, unique to Lincoln, is probably a medieval device to give a sense of forward movement towards the east. Known as crazy vaulting, it is the earliest example in Europe of tierceron vaulting, where not all of the ribs are structurally necessary. In Lincoln's example each keystone receives two ribs from one side and one from the other, the uneven effect, which ➤ p.90

A CHORISTER'S DAY

The life of a chorister in the 21st century is full and active. They all assemble each weekday morning for an hour-long rehearsal in the Song School at 8 am. During this they will practise all the music for the day, as well as beginning some of the dozen or more pieces that will be required at the weekend. After this they join their colleagues in Lincoln Minster School for the first lesson of the busy school day. A full day's academic and sporting activities follows. After school they usually return to the cathedral for afternoon tea

Clockwise from the top: Evensong; boy choristers rehearsing; girl choristers before a service; rehearsal in the song school.

followed by another rehearsal at 4.30 pm and then Evensong at 5.30 pm. The boys' and girls' sections of the choir generally alternate, each doing two weekday Evensongs and a share of the weekend's four choral services. If they are singing at Evensong, the children are generally not free until after 6.15 pm, which leaves minimal time for supper, homework and TV, so usually the children become adept at organizing their time in order to accommodate hobbies and other interests.

Children usually join the choir at the age of about nine and serve several months on a reduced timetable as probationers, during which they learn to sing, to sight-read and how to pronounce the different languages in which their music is written. Once they have achieved the required standard they are admitted as Burghersh chanters, receiving their white surplices or blue scapulars and the full responsibilities of choir membership. The four senior children appointed choristers wear the distinctive dark cloaks known as copes.

MUSIC AT LINCOLN CATHEDRAL

The precentor (first singer) is the canon responsible for the music and liturgy of the cathedral, and Peter Guerno, the first precentor, was appointed in 1092. It is not known at what stage a choir of boys and men was formed, but its continued existence was assured by an endowment by Bishop Alexander in 1148, setting up a school of singing. Indeed, the name of the village of Ashby Puerorum near Horncastle is derived from a later grant of land by Bishop Oliver Sutton (*puerorum* meaning 'of the boys'). In the Middle Ages the choir's workload was very heavy, with up to 10 sung services each day.

The choir, which successive bishops endowed, has been directed by many famous musicians, of whom the most illustrious was William Byrd, organist and master of the choristers from 1563 to 1572. Byrd later went on to be organist of the Chapel Royal. Apart from the period of the Civil War and Commonwealth (1643–59), there has been a choir or choirs at the cathedral since the 12th century, and since 1995 this has included girl choristers as well as boys. Today

Plaque in Minster Yard.

Right: Burghersh chanters in an Easter service.

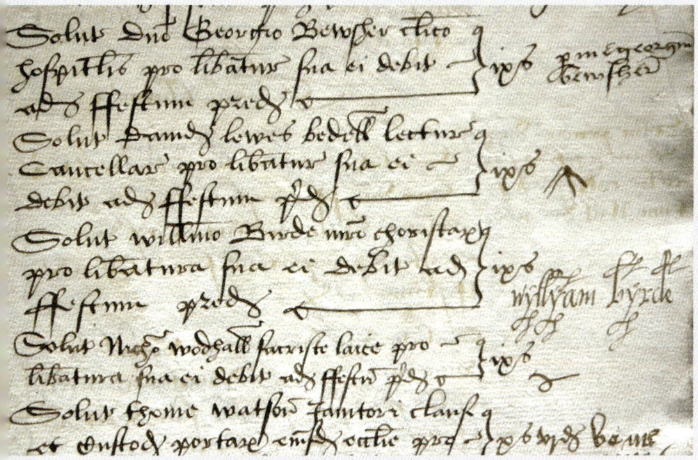

Signature of William Byrd in a cathedral account book, 1566.

we have 20 boys, 20 girls and nine singing men (lay vicars or choral scholars).

The children are known as Burghersh chanters and chantresses, with the four seniors in each section being choristers. Between them they sing eight choral services each week, as well as giving concerts and recitals in this country and abroad. They are trained by the directors of music and educated at Lincoln Minster School.

The cathedral's musical tradition is echoed in the carvings in the Angel Choir, which show angels playing a variety of musical instruments.

Right: the choir at Evensong.

The Judgement Porch.

THE JUDGEMENT PORCH

The position of the Judgement Porch at Lincoln is unusual. Of French origin, in most cases such porches were placed at the west end of churches as, for example, at Compostella. Lincoln is unique among English cathedrals in having such a porch at all and, among those cathedrals that do, for having it as the south porch of the Angel Choir. The reason is probably that the Angel Choir was nearing completion when such porches came into vogue, and it was added as a later refinement.

The idea is to remind the pilgrims on their way to visit the shrine of St Hugh of the options facing every human being, from the company of the saints in glory to the torments of the damned in hell. These are depicted most graphically around the central statue of Christ seated in judgement above the jaws of hell. The wise and the foolish bridesmaids are represented in the tympanum as are six kings and six queens, and either side of the door the Jewish and Christian faiths are personified as female statues. Known as *Synagoga* and *Ecclesia*, the former is blindfolded and the implied judgement is ironic at the entrance of the shrine to the saint who was famous for his protection of the Jewish people. The statue of Mother and Child is a 20th-century replacement of an earlier depiction. The statues further to the east of a king and queen probably represent Edward I and Eleanor of Castile, who were present at the consecration of the Angel Choir in 1280.

has been likened to the motion of a pair of scissors, impelling the eye forwards, towards the altar and the shrine behind.

The sanctuary contains the high altar, the table at which the Eucharist is celebrated. The original furnishings were destroyed at the Reformation and replaced with a wooden table, placed lengthways, and wooden wainscoting around the sanctuary perimeter. The current stone screen, carved reredos and altar were restored in 1769 and are based on the architecture of the tomb of Bishop de Luda in Ely Cathedral. The large central niche of the reredos was originally the frame for two paintings, the latter of which, depicting the Annunciation (when Mary was asked by the archangel to become the mother of Jesus), currently hangs in the north choir transept.

The graceful lines of the Angel Choir.

Detail of the high altar in the sanctuary.

On the north side of the sanctuary the six canopied niches date from about 1300. The three on the left are believed to be the tomb of Bishop Remigius, the founder of the cathedral in 1072, and those on the right form an Easter Sepulchre. This was a representation of the tomb of Christ, used for certain Holy Week ceremonies in the medieval period. Sleeping soldiers are carved underneath the sepulchre which, like the pulpitum, is intricately carved in the Decorated style with traces visible of its original paint.

The sanctuary forms the first two bays of the Angel Choir. St Hugh was canonized only 20 years after his death, and by 1255 it was decided that a special area was required for a shrine. The existing east end of the cathedral was pulled down and replaced by a five-bay extension. This was built in the new Geometric style, with more complicated window carving and yet more representation of foliage. The key thing to note, however, are the carvings of angels, which give the area its name. What the angels are doing gives us a real clue as to the way the medieval mind saw this part of the building. Those angels in the two bays of the high sanctuary are judging human beings: Adam and Eve are being expelled from the Garden of Eden, an angel is judging souls with a pair of scales and the instruments of Christ's passion are being displayed. This points to the Eucharist, the main activity celebrated in the sanctuary, as not only the meeting-point between earth and heaven, where Christ's sacrifice on the cross is participated in by the faithful in bread and wine, but also a point of 'crisis' where, as St Paul says, those who eat and drink unworthily call down judgement upon themselves.

To the right of the altar is the chantry of Katherine Swynford who was mistress and later wife of John of Gaunt. They married in the cathedral in 1396.

KATHERINE SWYNFORD

Katherine Swynford was the daughter of Payne de Roet, a Flemish knight who was in the retinue of Edward III's wife Philippa of Hainault. She married Hugh Swynford, a knight from the Lincolnshire manor of Kettlethorpe, while she was in her early teens, and she bore him, probably, three children. She became the sister-in-law of Geoffrey Chaucer when he married Philippa de Roet. Appointed to the household of Blanche, wife of John of Gaunt, duke of Lancaster, in 1369, Katherine ministered to her when she died at Bolingbroke later that year. Katherine's husband Hugh died two years later, after which she returned as governess to the two daughters of John of Gaunt. She became John's mistress for many years, bearing him four illegitimate children, to whom were given the surname Beaufort: John, 1st earl of Somerset; Henry, Cardinal Beaufort and one time bishop of Lincoln; Thomas, 1st duke of Exeter; and Joan, countess of Westmoreland.

For some time Katherine resided at the property that is now the deanery in Minster Yard. Following the death of his second wife, John married Katherine in the cathedral on 13 January 1396. He died three years later, Katherine herself dying on 10 May 1403. She is buried on the south side of the sanctuary of the cathedral, together with her daughter Joan who died in 1440. Katherine, the great-great-grandmother of the future Henry VII, and Joan are both seen as women who wielded considerable power in a patriarchal society, able to transcend the social conventions and even legal prescriptions of their day.

David Vale's reconstruction of Minster Yard as it may have looked in the 14th century when Katherine lived in what is now the deanery.

Adam and Eve are expelled from the Garden of Eden. Detail of carving in the high sanctuary.

Christ seated, wearing the Crown of Thorns and displaying the wound in His side. A small angel brings a soul in a napkin.

Farthest east, beyond the sanctuary, is St Hugh's Shrine, the easternmost three bays built to house the body of the bishop responsible for rebuilding the cathedral in 1192. It is thought that the carvings here reflect the so-called Laudate Psalms (148, 149 and 150), which form the conclusion of the medieval morning office of Lauds. They speak of praising God upon the timbrel, the lyre, the trumpet, the harp, the strings, the pipe and the cymbals, and such instruments can be seen in the hands of the angels in these bays. St Hugh was originally buried elsewhere in his cathedral, but re-interred in a magnificent shrine at the east end on 6 October 1280 in the presence of King Edward I and Queen Eleanor. Pilgrims flocked to his shrine until the Reformation. His head was separated from his body during the process of re-interment and venerated on the intricately carved plinth, which still stands, though the tomb containing his body was destroyed in the 16th century. The 1986 sculpture by David Poston over the site of the head shrine reminds us of Hugh's tame swan at his manor of Stow, which has become his symbol.

Opposite: a pause for conversation in the Angel Choir.

The Lincoln Imp.

This easternmost section of the building is the culmination of the pilgrim's journey through the cathedral. Just as the font stands at the beginning of the journey, so the shrine of a saint believed to be in heaven marks its end. The richness of colour and carving speak of the glory that awaits the Christian after death. However, humour and mischief are still present. At the top of the pillar closest to the head shrine you will find the carving known as the Lincoln Imp. This is a little stone devil, feathered but with horns and hooves, one leg crossed over the other. There are differing legends about how he came to be here, but the most common seems to be that in the 14th century Satan sent two imps down to earth to do evil work. Initially the two imps went to Chesterfield, where they sat on the church spire twisting it into its current shape. After vandalizing the spire at Chesterfield the two imps headed to Lincoln Cathedral. When they arrived, the devil instructed them to cause as much mayhem as possible. They began by smashing up tables and chairs and tripping up the bishop, and then they started destroying the Angel Choir. An angel appeared and told them to stop. The braver of the two imps started to throw rocks at the angel, but the other imp cowered under the broken tables and chairs. The angel turned the first imp to stone and placed him high above a pillar, which gave the second imp a chance to escape. Whatever the truth of these legends, the figure has become much loved in Lincolnshire and served as the county emblem for many years.

View in 1816–17 of the tombs of Bishop Henry Burghersh and of Robert Burghersh, his father, with reconstruction of canopies from surviving fragments by D. T. Powell and E. J. Willson. From a manuscript in the possession of Lord Monson (by kind permission of the Trustees of the 10th Baron Monson).

Near to the shrine is a series of chantry chapels where prayers could be offered for deceased patrons. Different crafts are represented: pottery in the Burghersh Chantry on the north side, where the Gilbert Pots by Robin Welch reflect the local saint Gilbert of Sempringham. Gilbert was a contemporary of St Hugh, a priest of the diocese who founded the only distinctively English religious order, that of the Gilbertine Canons. Gilbert's order was unique in that he had male and female canons living on opposite sides of a common church, a wall dividing the two houses. He is reputed to have been a hunchback, which is reflected in the misshapen character of the pots, the largest which it is possible to throw on a wheel.

On the south side the wool trade is represented by the Duncan Grant murals, which decorate the Russell Chantry. John Russell was bishop of Lincoln between 1480 and 1494, Lord Chancellor to Richard III and one of England's best educated men. He built this chantry at his own expense to house his tomb. Both the Cantilupe Chantry at the southeast end of the cathedral and the Burghersh Chantry have significant medieval stained glass work. The Fleming Chantry was built to house the tomb of Richard Fleming, and the splendour of that bishop of Lincoln in life is contrasted with his decaying corpse in death. A medieval rhyme, *Memento mori*, comes to mind:

As once I was
So are you now
As now I am
So shall you be!

Duncan Grant in 1912.

From the top: Lincoln quay in the 15th century; Pied wagtails, detail; self portrait by Duncan Grant.

DUNCAN GRANT

The setting-up of the Edward Austin Abbey Memorial Trust allowed the dean and chapter to commission the established mural-artist Duncan Grant to decorate a rather dull chantry chapel on the southeast side of the cathedral dedicated to St Blaise. Blaise is the patron saint of wool-workers, probably because he is thought to have been tortured by carding (dragged over something resembling a garden rake) before being beheaded in the early 4th century. This association led Grant to design murals along medieval lines but in a modern idiom, on the theme of the Good Shepherd. Jesus is portrayed as a young, beardless man rather in the Greek style, carrying a lamb across his shoulders. He is standing in a minora (lozenge of light) in a field of sheep-shearers, who pause from their work to recognize the Christ among them. On the facing wall is a scene of Lincoln quay in the 15th century with workers loading wool bales while women look on, and over the chapel door is a depiction of St Blaise. The colours are vibrant and exuberant.

Grant's association with the controversial Bloomsbury Group, his conscientious objection during the First World War and his rather complicated private life, believed by many to be reflected in the murals, dogged this commission even before its unveiling in 1959, and for much of their life the murals have been locked away from view. Restoration work began on them in 1989, and they were opened to the public again in 1991.

THE CLOISTER AND CHAPTER HOUSE

BY NICHOLAS BENNETT

The cloister of Lincoln Cathedral is an enigma. For a medieval monastic house, the cloister provided a hub for the activities of the community, expressed at various times in liturgy, contemplation and reading. It provided a means of access between the different buildings that made up the monastic complex: refectory and kitchen, dormitory and infirmary. Having typically two doorways connecting it with the church, it provided a route for processions. The garth (central area) provided a green space in the heart of the monastic enclosure; as a 12th-century writer put it: 'The green lawn of the cloister refreshes the eyes of beholders and brings to their minds the delightfulness of Paradise.'

The Chapter House roof.

Lincoln Cathedral, of course, was a secular (non-monastic) foundation, so that much of the rationale for building a cloister was absent. Nevertheless, it is striking to note that, of the nine medieval English secular cathedrals, all save two (Lichfield and York) had cloisters. Some of these took up the idea of a cloister comparatively late in their existence. The two-storey South Cloister at St Paul's Cathedral, one of the earliest examples of the Perpendicular style, was begun in 1332, and the chapter was evidently so pleased with it that a second cloister was constructed on the north side of the nave early in the following century. At Hereford the building of the cloister was begun in the late 14th century in order to provide a link with the new chapter house, but in the event only the east and south walks were completed. Chichester's cloister belongs entirely to the 15th century, its irregular plan dictated by the boundaries of existing buildings.

These late examples suggest that a cloister remained an integral part of the concept of a secular cathedral. Many foundations of secular canons looked back to the 'rule' of Chrodegang, the 8th-century bishop of Metz, for their inspiration. Chrodegang held that where the endowment of a church was used for the support of a group of clergy, and, especially where that group constituted the household of a bishop, they should live in common and the bishop should provide for their common maintenance and build them a cloister. How far did this ideal of the common life prevail in the secular cathedrals founded in the late 11th century?

Our knowledge of the organization of secular cathedrals derives to a large extent from the written evidence of statutes and act books from the 13th and 14th centuries. The picture given by these sources is one of largely independent chapters, their canons living in

Opposite: 'On sunny days, Italy at Lincoln is quite a reality.'

The new chancellor is installed as a member of the College of Canons.

separate houses allotted to their use, with the bishop taking little part in their affairs. It is important not to transpose these conditions back into the murkier waters of the poorly documented 11th and 12th centuries. One reason why bishops like Remigius of Lincoln and Osmund of Salisbury chose secular foundations for their cathedrals was the need to provide for the large numbers of clerks required to administer their extensive dioceses. The early years of these foundations involved a much closer relationship between the bishop and the clerks of his household who made up the chapter. It was only gradually, as the 12th century progressed, that the common life of the episcopal *familia* broke up, as pastoral responsibilities drew the bishop out into the diocese, while liturgical duties kept the chapter fixed in residence at the cathedral.

The pioneers of the secular cathedral cloister in this country were Wells and Salisbury. At the former the 11th-century Bishop Giso established a chapter of canons following a common life. Although the cloister and refectory he built for them were demolished by his successor, the desire to secure cathedral status for Wells in the face of determined competition from Bath Abbey prompted a succession of building programmes of mounting aspiration. A new cloister was built in the mid-12th century by Bishop Robert, and this in turn was replaced by a successor during the 13th-century rebuilding programme. At Old Sarum the community of canons established by Bishop Osmund was noted for its scholarship, which is reflected in the remarkable collection of manuscripts surviving from his episcopate. Given this close relationship between bishop and canons, it is not surprising to discover that the building by the powerful Bishop Roger of a new east end to the existing cathedral, completed by 1126, had already allowed for the addition of a cloister connecting it with the bishop's palace to the northeast. This cloister, whose foundations can still be seen, was constructed in the mid-12th century.

At Lincoln life in the household of the early bishops appears to have been characterized by splendour rather than by scholarship. The historian Henry of Huntingdon, who was educated among the clerks of Bishop Robert Bloet, leaves us in no doubt of the lavish episcopal lifestyle. Here again, the impression is one of a close-knit community, whose links included the ties of family as well as those of a common purpose. Henry himself was the son of Archdeacon

The elegant and daring flying buttresses outside the chapter house.

Nicholas of Huntingdon. Bishop Bloet's successor, Alexander the Magnificent, was himself the nephew of Bishop Roger of Salisbury whose (probable) son, Adelelm, became dean of Lincoln in the 1140s. Alexander's brother Nigel also attained the episcopate as bishop of Ely, and shortly before he achieved this rank he had a son, Richard Fitz Nigel, who himself became dean of Lincoln in the 1180s. Such links served to uphold something of the ideal of bishop and chapter sharing in a common purpose, in face of the relentless forces driving them apart. With this in mind, and with the examples of Wells and Salisbury to be emulated, it is not a complete surprise to find that the idea of a cloister was in the minds of the chapter in the 1180s.

A charter, preserved in the cathedral archives and dating from late 1183 or early 1184, refers to a piece of land in the parish of All Saints in the Bail, adjoining the gate of the 'Bedern'. This word, which means 'a house of prayer', was used at York and Beverley for the college of the vicars choral, although it is unlikely that this represented the use of the Lincoln building as early as 1184. At the same time, the acquisition of individual houses by the canons was in its infancy. When Richard Fitz Neal came to Lincoln as dean in 1184 he found that there was no deanery and took steps to secure a suitable residence for this purpose. The Bedern, therefore, may have been a building provided for the common life of such canons and other ministers of the cathedral who had not at that point obtained separate dwellings. This possibility is strengthened by the further reference in the 1184 charter that the land in question could, if it was thought necessary, be used for building a cloister.

The date of this charter coincides exactly with the brief episcopate of Walter of Coutances (1183–4), a man who subsequently, as archbishop of Rouen, oversaw the reconstruction of that cathedral in the same way that Hugh did at Lincoln. The canons there remembered him as 'a magnificent benefactor of the church'. It would have been entirely in character for him, arriving in Lincoln for his enthronement on 11 December 1183, to have proposed the building of a cloister in order to bring his cathedral up to the standard of Salisbury and Wells. The site of the proposed cloister cannot be known with any certainty, but the situation of the land in the parish of All Saints in the Bail suggests that it lay in the area northwest of the cathedral. The plan may have been to build a cloister on the north side of the nave, a position occupied by the great cloister at Canterbury, perhaps linking the cathedral with the Bedern itself.

Lincoln's 'lost cloister' was never built. Bishop Walter was translated to the archbishopric of Rouen and had left Lincoln by December 1184. The following year, on Palm Sunday, the cathedral suffered catastrophic damage in an earthquake. When Hugh of Avalon was enthroned as the next bishop in 1186, the priority was to rebuild the church. Nevertheless, although the cloister was forgotten for a time, its eventual construction came about as a direct result of the layout of the new cathedral inaugurated by St Hugh in 1192.

The first stage towards the building of the cloister at Lincoln was the building of the chapter house. This was in progress around 1220 when *The Metrical Life of St Hugh* recorded that it rivalled Solomon's temple in its stonework and architecture. It is thought to have been completed before the death of Bishop Hugh of Wells in 1235.

Opposite: detail of the cloister roof.

To gain access to the building, a pentice (covered walkway) was erected, leading from the northeast transept. This walkway appears to have continued past the chapter house entrance, following the line of the old Roman wall, and it provided the east walk of the cloister. In 1296 Bishop Oliver Sutton reported to the dean, Philip Willoughby, that he had given permission for the chapter to build the southern walk of the cloister and that they now sought to construct the northern side 'over the wall of the dean's stable, which is built upon the church's ground'. Sutton himself gave 50 marks towards the completion of the project.

Sutton's letter clearly implies that the building of the deanery stables had encroached in some way on the cathedral's land. This boundary issue continued to cause problems, and in 1437 Dean Mackworth was accused, among other things, of taking down part of the cloister and using some of the stone to build a stable over its north wall. Bishop Alnwick ordered the dean either to remove the stable or to pay a rent for it. Whether it was as a result of this dispute, or through the later ravages and neglect of the civil wars and interregnum of the mid-17th century, the north walk of the cloister had suffered so much damage by 1674 that it was described as ruinous. Dean Honywood's solution was to use the site for the building of the Wren library.

The existence of the deanery stables on the northern boundary of the cloister resulted in a layout that was rectangular rather than the ideal square. The original design, before the north walk was replaced by the Wren library, consisted of 14 bays on the north and south sides and 10 bays on the west and east. These pleasing proportions are enhanced by the uniformity of style and of spacing in the arcade screens. The naturalistic decoration, both in the stone tracery and in the wooden bosses, where foliage, animals and scenes from daily life predominate over more strictly religious themes, provide a setting that is spiritually as well as physically external to the cathedral itself. So although the cloister, by the time it was built, had little to do with liturgy or access to other buildings, it could nevertheless provide a space for recreation and contemplation for clergy, clerks and choristers amid the demanding liturgical duties of the cathedral's daily routine.

Minster schoolchildren perform a lunchtime concert in the chapter house.

Ironically perhaps, the cloister today provides more of a focus for the day-to-day activities of the cathedral community than it can ever have done in the Middle Ages. It provides access not only to the chapter house but to the library, refectory and lavatories. Children from the Minster School process regularly around its walks to and from their assemblies. Summer visitors to the cathedral find in it a space for contemplation, where they can pause to absorb their impressions of this magnificent building, particularly as they gaze up at the awe-inspiring central tower, seated beneath the light Tuscan arcades of Sir Christopher Wren's library, where, as John Harris so aptly put it, 'on sunny days, Italy at Lincoln is quite a reality'.

The chapter house, which had provided the original impetus for the construction of the cloister, is entered through a doorway in the centre of the east walk. The building is in two parts, with a passage of two bays leading to the chapter house itself, a spacious 10-sided polygon with a central column. It is an early and influential example of the ➤ p.104

GOVERNANCE

The chapter house stands as a symbol of the authority by which the cathedral is governed. In the post-Conquest period, when Remigius transferred the see from Dorchester to Lincoln, the prevailing model for cathedral foundations, promoted especially by Archbishop Lanfranc, was monastic. Canterbury, Winchester, Norwich and Durham all emerged as Benedictine houses under the rule of a prior. Remigius, though himself a monk, saw a different need in Lincoln. The vast size of the diocese required a body of administrators and lawyers to ensure its smooth running, and he therefore created a chapter of secular canons, each endowed with a prebend or source of income deriving from manorial lands or ecclesiastical tithes. Seven archdeacons were also appointed, and, at the apex of the structure, were three dignitaries: a treasurer to oversee the services, a precentor in charge of the music and, over all the others, a dean to act as the president of chapter.

Remigius builds a new cathedral. Detail from window in the chapter house.

Remigius created 21 prebends, and his successor, Robert Bloet, doubled the number. Two new dignitaries were added in the 12th century: a subdean (1133) to act as the dean's deputy and a chancellor (1148) to look after the schools and the library. By the late 13th century there were 56 prebends, their endowments scattered across the diocese and beyond, a geographical spread vividly illustrated by the tablets on the stalls in St Hugh's Choir.

By this date, however, the original model of the cathedral structure had begun to break down. The foundation, which had been created to provide for members of the episcopal household, gradually became more independent as successive bishops spent more and more time travelling around the huge diocese. The dean and chapter took increasing responsibility for the running of the cathedral, and a distinction grew up between those canons who resided permanently in Lincoln and those whose duties kept them away from the mother church, some serving the bishop in the diocese, some serving the king or other lords. Those who stayed in Lincoln were entitled to a share in the revenues of the common fund, and houses of increasingly impressive stature were provided for them in Minster Yard.

As the cathedral grew into independence, the need arose for a codification of the rules governing the rights and responsibilities of its members. These rules combined a body of unwritten customs with written statutes. By 1214 this process was sufficiently advanced for a written statement of the Lincoln customs to be sent to the newly founded chapter of Moray as a model. About 1330 it appears that a decision was made to draw up a register of the customs of Lincoln. This volume, known from its binding as the *Liber Niger* (Black Book), became recognized as the chief repository of the written statutes of the cathedral.

The notorious and protracted dispute of the early 15th century between Dean Mackworth and the residentiary canons was concluded by the *Laudum* (award) issued by Bishop Alnwick in 1439. Observing that the dispute had

Meeting of the Chapter.

become exacerbated through the confused state of the statutes, the bishop offered to draw up a new code, the *Novum Registrum*. He based this on the statutes in use at St Paul's Cathedral. The attempted imposition of this code succeeded (where all else had failed) in uniting the dean and canons – in their opposition to the scheme. Although the *Novum Registrum* was discussed at 40 chapter meetings, it was never approved.

At the Reformation, the monastic cathedrals of England were transformed into cathedrals of the new foundation and received broadly similar sets of statutes from the Crown. Lincoln, however, continued to be governed in accordance with the customs that had evolved between the 11th and 15th centuries, although their liturgical provisions were no longer observed. It was not until 1936 that Lincoln came into line with other cathedrals in being governed by a body of statutes issued by the Crown. The 20th-century statutes combined an awareness of the history and constitution of the cathedral with the changes introduced by recent Cathedrals Measures. They forged a closer link between the bishop and his cathedral, setting out his right to celebrate Holy Communion and to preach there, and to use the cathedral for ordinations, confirmations and other special occasions.

In 1990 the Care of Cathedrals Measure introduced a Cathedrals Fabric Commission for England, with a Fabric Advisory Committee for each cathedral. The Cathedrals Measure of 1999 required all cathedrals to produce a new constitution and statutes. Those for Lincoln came into operation on 17 November (St Hugh's Day) 2000. Among other changes, these statutes introduced a new Cathedral Council to review and advise on the work of the chapter.

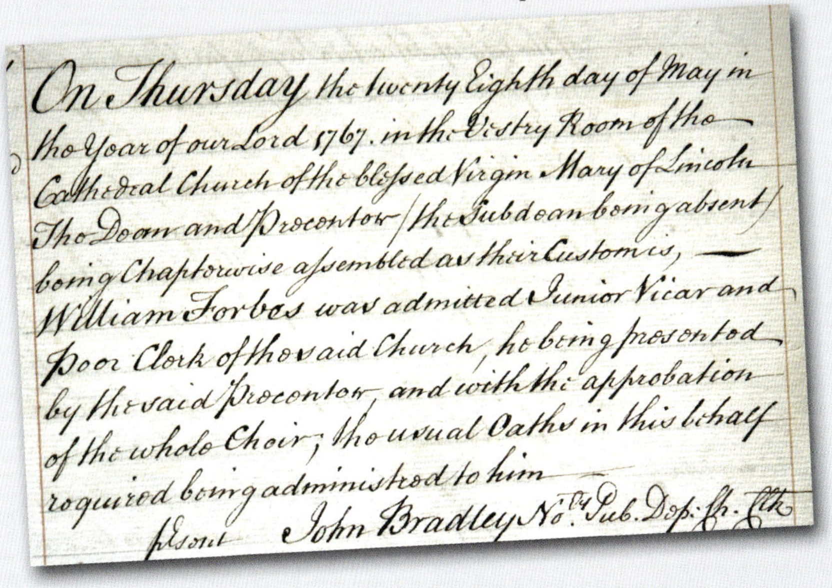
On Thursday the twenty Eighth day of May in the Year of our Lord 1767. in the Vestry Room of the Cathedral Church of the blessed Virgin Mary of Lincoln The Dean and Precentor (the Subdean being absent) being Chapterwise assembled as their Custom is, — William Forbes was admitted Junior Vicar and Poor Clerk of the said Church, he being presented by the said Precentor and with the approbation of the whole Choir, the usual Oaths in this behalf required being administred to him

Present John Bradley No. Pub. Dep. Ch. Clk

Below: notes of a chapter meeting in 1767.

The rose window in the chapter house.

centrally planned polygonal chapter house that became a feature of later English Gothic cathedrals. The vault, radiating outwards from the central pillar, arches overhead like a 10-pointed star. This lavish architectural setting served to emphasize the importance of the chapter and its deliberations in the life of the cathedral. It also provided a daily focus for the common worship of the medieval cathedral community.

Each morning after the service of Prime, the choir and chapter withdrew to the chapter house and took up their places around the central pillar. One of the boys, normally the thurifer, stood at a desk to read out a passage from the *Martiloge* (martyrology), giving the liturgical details of the morrow, the list of saints to be commemorated and the names of those past members of the foundation or its benefactors, whose obits or anniversaries were to be observed. The names of those due to act as readers or as singers were read out and another lesson was read. Then all those present withdrew for the chapter mass, except on Saturdays, when the canons would remain behind for the business of the weekly chapter meeting.

Larger gatherings of the cathedral foundation assembled in the chapter house from time to time. One such occasion was during a vacancy in the deanery, when notice would be given to the dignitaries, the archdeacons and all the canons dwelling in England to assemble at Lincoln on a certain day, for the purpose of electing a dean. Once the election had taken place in due form and the person elected had been presented to the bishop for his approval, the dean-elect would be led from the chapter house to the high altar, while the *Te Deum* was sung. After his installation, the new dean would return to the chapter house, where all the canons and other ministers would promise obedience to him, as dean. Similarly, a new canon wishing to be installed would first be admitted by the dean in the chapter house, where he would take the oath to observe the customs of the cathedral, and then, after he had been placed in his stall in the choir, he would return to the chapter house to promise obedience to the dean.

The benefits of the prayers of the cathedral body were extended to a wider circle of benefactors known as the confraternity. The existence of this company can be seen as early as the 12th century in the names of those included in the obit roll copied into the Chapter Bible. By the 14th century a ceremony of admission to the confraternity had evolved. On 27 March 1387, in what was no doubt a dazzling ceremony, Richard II and his queen, Anne of Bohemia, were welcomed to the chapter house by the bishop and chapter and duly admitted to the company of brothers and sisters of the cathedral church of Lincoln. At a similar occasion the previous year, the king's uncle John of Gaunt had been present to witness the admission of his son (the future Henry IV) together with Thomas, the son of his mistress Katherine Swynford, and Philippa Chaucer, Katherine's sister and the wife of the poet. All such members of the confraternity were received as partners of the cathedral body and partakers in its prayers, suffrages, fastings, pilgrimages, alms and other meritorious works of mercy done by day or night in this holy place.

Opposite: the cloister is at the heart of day-to-day activities in the cathedral.

Above: Cloister garth at night.

Right: door into the chapter house.

Because of its size, the chapter house was also used for other assemblies besides those of the cathedral foundation. Notable among these were the Parliaments held in Lincoln in the 14th century. That which was summoned to meet in the city by Edward II in 1316 is known to have used the chapter house for some of its sessions, and it would seem likely that this also happened during the first Lincoln Parliament held by Edward I in 1301. The impact of such an assembly would have been considerable, as bishops and abbots, earls and barons, knights and burgesses converged on the city from all corners of England. The sheriff was ordered to supply 400 quarters of wheat, 400 quarters of malt, 1,000 quarters of oats, sufficient hay to feed 400 horses for a month, 100 oxen and cows, 100 pigs and 300 sheep for the provisioning of this multitude. The influx of several hundred people into the city must have strained the resources of accommodation, even though it no doubt provided a windfall for local innkeepers.

Other gatherings that took place in the chapter house were of a more sombre nature. In 1310 some of the knights of the suppressed order of the Templars were tried here. The break with Rome engineered by Henry VIII to facilitate his marriage with Anne Boleyn was effected, so far as Lincoln cathedral was concerned, in the chapter house on Wednesday, 5 August 1534. On that day, the entire body of the cathedral clergy – 72 men in all – assembled there formally to subscribe their names to the Act of Parliament that made Henry supreme head of the Church in England and repudiated the authority of the pope, or the 'bishop of Rome' as he was henceforth to be known. The dean and precentor signed first, followed by the chancellor and the other dignitaries. Then came the sacrist, succentor and vice-chancellor, and these were followed by 13 vicars-choral who also held chantries, five vicars who had no chantry and nearly 30 chantry priests who were not vicars. Finally, and no doubt bemused by the whole business (having struggled, we may imagine, with the Latin text of the Act), came the nine poor clerks.

Henry's reformation did not meet with enthusiasm in all quarters and, just two years later, the chapter house witnessed the crucial stages of the Lincolnshire Rising. Having arrived in Lincoln en masse, the commons sent out parties to bring in the local gentry. As negotiations went on to draw up the articles of grievances, meetings were held in the chapter house and elsewhere. The climax came on the afternoon of Tuesday, 10 October, when 300 of the commons came to the gentry assembled in the chapter house, accompanied by a messenger bearing the king's reply. The commons demanded that this letter be read out. The recorder of Lincoln, Thomas Moigne, did so, but he omitted one passage, which he feared might arouse the wrath of the commons. This may have been the king's well-known reference to the county as 'one of the most brute and beastly of the whole realm'. His omission was noticed, and some of the commons withdrew to the cloister where they planned to kill Moigne and some others as they came out through the west door. The intended victims were smuggled out through the south door and taken to safety in the chancery.

As the reformation progressed, more and more aspects of traditional religion were abolished. The replacement of the medieval liturgy by the English Prayer Book in 1549 brought to an end the daily readings from the *Martiloge* in the chapter house. Thereafter the obits of members of the cathedral foundation went unrecorded until the practice was reintroduced, as part of daily Evensong, by Dean Dunlop in 1952. The chapter house continued to be used for the admission of dignitaries and canons, but in general the 17th and 18th centuries were a period of neglect for this part of the building.

It was the reformers of the late Victorian period who brought new life to the cathedral. The restoration of the chapter house in 1889–90 included the levelling ('for the

Part of the 'timeline' window outside the new lavatories.

THE NEW LAVATORIES

BY PHILIP BUCKLER

The most recent addition to the cathedral has been one of the most welcome – the provision of proper lavatory facilities. Many a concert-goer may recall the frustration and discomfort of lengthy queues for limited facilities in times past.

It was a relief to all when the new lavatories were opened early in 2009. Built using the skills of the Cathedral Works Department on a site between the cloister and the nave known as the Nettleyard – where herbs may have been grown for medicinal purposes in medieval times – the building uses Lincolnshire limestone from the cathedral quarry to match the main fabric of the cathedral. On two floors housing additional facilities upstairs to cater for the larger occasions, one of the main features is a stained glass window, two storeys high, designed and made by our glaziers and displaying a timeline of the cathedral's history.

High on the walls of the staircase are displayed two pieces of medieval carving, set on corbels of contemporary carving based on designs submitted for a competition by the people of Lincoln. One shows two swans (a swan being the emblem of St Hugh) framing the West Front of the cathedral. The other displays the fruits of the agricultural life of Lincolnshire. Both corbels have been not only carved by cathedral masons, but also painted by them in accordance with the medieval tradition.

To the medieval cathedral was added the library in the 17th century and its extension in the 20th century. The new lavatories are the first contribution of our 21st century.

Deep in conversation in the cloister.

convenience of placing chairs') of the pavement, which had previously sloped gradually from the circumference up to the central pillar. There were inevitably those who deplored the loss of this 'curious and unique feature' of the building, but it was undeniable that the change opened up the use of the room for organizations such as the Diocesan Conference, which was thus enabled to transfer its annual meeting here, in place of the more worldly surroundings of the Lincoln Assembly Rooms.

At the same time, an imaginative scheme for replacing the chapter house windows with stained glass illustrating the history of the cathedral was in progress. The medieval oak throne was moved from its home in the library, given a new canopy and placed in a position of honour in the chapter house. This change was so successful that it was soon believed that it had always stood there and that it had been provided specially for the use of Edward I at the 1301 Parliament. A detailed examination of its construction made by Charles Tracy, however, indicates that it was made in the 1330s, and it has been convincingly identified as the medieval episcopal throne removed from St Hugh's Choir during Essex's alterations in the 1778.

Today the chapter house is regularly used for a variety of events. The annual meeting of the College of Canons takes place here each November on St Hugh's Day. This is the occasion of the installation of new canons, a service that retains many of its traditional elements, as when the new members come in procession to the chapter house at the conclusion of Evensong to be welcomed into the College and to promise obedience to the dean. The Association of Friends holds its annual meeting here in the summer. There are regular exhibitions and lunchtime concerts. A regular programme of lectures is offered, including the annual Grosseteste Lecture, which is given by a distinguished speaker. The provision of catering facilities has enabled a variety of convivial gatherings to take place here, so that a visitor to the chapter house might find preparations under way for the annual harvest supper or the Cathedral Community Association's Shrove Tuesday party. The chapter house today is at the heart of the life of the community.

CLOISTER BOSSES

Although the wooden vaults of the cloister were renewed during J.L. Pearson's restoration of 1883–92, they are decorated with the original carved bosses from the late 13th century. Many have suffered damage, but enough remains to demonstrate their superb craftsmanship. Close study of these intricate carvings opens a window for us into the world of medieval Lincolnshire. Amid the naturalistic foliage – mostly oak and vine leaves – can be seen dogs and oxen, lions and dragons, a winged ape, a hare wearing a jerkin, griffins and other creatures from the Bestiary. An incomplete series of the labours of the months, unparalleled elsewhere in the Gothic sculpture of England, includes figures of a man sowing (October), another man killing a pig (November), his axe raised as the animal forages among leaves and acorns, and a third man feasting (December), a cask and jug within easy reach.

Other secular figures can be seen – a man caressing the face of a woman, a musician playing the bagpipes, a woman with a wimple and a man with toothache. In contrast with this worldly imagery, there is a small group of religious subjects, notably in the southern half of the east walk. In the southeast corner a bishop, vested and enthroned, is succeeded by the Coronation of the Virgin. Beyond this is a representation of the Virgin seated, the Child on her lap holding a small bird, with a dove behind. Finally, immediately outside the chapter house, is the figure of Christ enthroned.

Clockwise from the top: a man sowing(October); another man killing a pig(November); a third man feasting(December); a musician playing the bagpipes; man caressing the face of a woman; the Virgin seated, the Child on her lap.

THE LIBRARY

BY NICHOLAS BENNETT

The Lord crowns King David: initial 'D' from Psalm 109, in Peter Lombard's Commentary on the Psalter, c.*1200.*

A collection of books has been central to the cathedral's educational work from the beginning. When Remigius moved the seat of his bishopric to Lincoln after 1072 it is likely that he brought at least one manuscript volume – the late 10th-century copy of the Homilies of the Venerable Bede – to form the nucleus of a library for the new foundation. As the work of the cathedral school developed its need for books grew. The magnificent Chapter Bible of *c.*1100 – the earliest English example of an illustrated Romanesque Bible – and a copy of Archbishop Lanfranc's collection of canon law texts, made at around the same date, are two of a small group of manuscripts probably commissioned for the new library from local scribes and bookbinders.

When Hamo became the cathedral's first chancellor in 1148, he was presented with a list of 44 books, kept in an *armarium* (cupboard), which thereafter became his responsibility. Hamo's list still survives, copied on to the flyleaf of the Chapter Bible. It shows that the growth of the library during the second half of the 12th century was the result of generous bequests from bishops, dignitaries and canons. Some of these gifts still survive in the collection, among them a beautifully illuminated commentary on the Psalms given by Chancellor Hamo himself. By 1200 the collection had grown to around a hundred volumes.

There were losses as well as gains. The cathedral canons had the right to borrow volumes from the *armarium*, and, in the way of library users down the ages, they did not always return them. Hamo's list records that one Master Gerard had given a copy of Vegetius' *On the Art of Warfare* to replace the classic work *On the Consolation of Philosophy* of Boethius, *quem perdiderat* (which he had lost). The system of lending evidently involved the lodging of a book of similar value in the *armarium* as a pledge. Over the decades more and more of the original gifts to the library were replaced by these pledges, so that by 1420, with the collection still at around a hundred manuscripts, only 40 of the 12th-century books survived.

The solution was to build a designated room for the library. In the early years of the 15th century other cathedrals, such as Wells and York, were doing the same thing. The

Opposite: drawing of an elephant in Conrad Gesner, Historiae Animalium, *1551.*

MAGNA CARTA AND THE CHARTER OF THE FOREST

Among the rich treasures in the archives of Lincoln Cathedral, none is so celebrated as the Magna Carta of 1215. Yet when King John and the rebel barons faced each other at Runnymede on 15 June 1215, neither side can have realized that the written truce they agreed on that day would ultimately achieve iconic status as a charter of liberties for nations across the world. There was deep distrust in both camps, and it was clear to many that the king had every intention of ditching the truce as soon as he could possibly do so.

But this was in the future. As soon as the agreement was concluded, its clauses were written out in a formal charter, and copies were made for distribution across the land. Of these copies, only four survive: two in the British Library, one at Salisbury and the document in Lincoln. The Lincoln copy is the only one of the four known – through its endorsement *Lincolnia* – to be in its original location.

Within a few weeks of Runnymede, King John repudiated the charter and fought back vigorously against his baronial opponents. His death in October 1216 dramatically changed the situation. The rebels now found themselves fighting against John's nine-year old son, Henry III, whose guardians took the unexpected move of reissuing Magna Carta, neatly wrong-footing the barons, some of whom crossed over to the king's side. The civil war culminated in the siege and battle of Lincoln in May 1217, when many of the rebels were captured.

At a council held in the autumn of 1217 Magna Carta was reissued for a second time. On this occasion the clauses dealing with the administration of the royal forests were expanded and embodied in a second document, the Charter of the Forest. Only two copies of this second charter survive, one of them again in the archives of Lincoln Cathedral.

Magna Carta and the Charter of the Forest did not in themselves solve the disputes between Crown and people, but throughout the remainder of the 13th century every time the king appeared to be pushing his authority to the limit the cry went up for the reissue of the charters, and by the end of the century they had been enshrined in the law of the land.

Although the majority of the clauses of Magna Carta were concerned with short-term disputes – the removal of foreign officials from government, the regulation of feudal payments – two of its clauses were of more general effect. These laid down that no free man was to be imprisoned except by the judgement of his equals or by the law of the land, and that the king was not to deny, or to sell, justice. It is these two clauses above all that have ensured for Magna Carta its iconic status as a charter of liberties.

The global significance of Magna Carta has now been recognized by the award of Memory of the World status by UNESCO. An ongoing programme of conservation monitoring is in place to ensure the preservation of this outstanding document for the benefit of future generations.

'LINCOLNIA': this contemporary endorsement shows that Lincoln Cathedral's copy of the 1215 Magna Carta remains in its original location.

traditional site for the library of an ecclesiastical foundation was above the east range of the cloister, and so it was in this corner of the cathedral building that the five-bay, timber-framed medieval library was completed in 1422. The room was furnished with oak lecterns, with benches attached. Each lectern was lit by a two-light window, with a larger window at each end of the building providing additional light. Access was probably by way of a stone newel staircase in the chapter house vestibule.

The manuscripts were now securely chained to the lecterns to prevent further losses. A new catalogue was made, listing 109 volumes, of which 88 survive in the collection today, a testimony to the efficacy of chaining books. The 15th-century library was almost entirely theological in content, keeping to its original purpose of being a working collection for the cathedral chapter. Here they could work in comfort (if not always in warmth), watched from above by ranks of graceful feathered angels along either side of the oak-timbered roof with its curiously carved bosses, as they turned the leaves of the mighty works of medieval scholarship, of Jerome, Augustine and Thomas Aquinas, of Peter Lombard and Gregory the Great.

The 15th-century catalogue was completed about the year 1455, ironically the same year in which Johann Gutenberg of Mainz produced his first printed Bible and the world of book production was turned upside down. The library continued to acquire manuscript volumes, but before long printed books began to arrive, claiming space on the oak lecterns. The collection began to multiply with these new accessions. Some came by the traditional means of gift or bequest; others came from the libraries of monasteries and other religious houses that were dissolved during the 1530s. To accommodate these books, additional shelves were constructed in the lower part of each lectern.

The medieval library, with manuscripts on display.

The Chapter Bible of c.1100: the beginning of the Book of Joshua.

ARCHIVES

The cathedral archives provide a rich resource for historians. The unrivalled series of royal charters, which includes Magna Carta itself (see p.112), begins with the writ issued by William the Conqueror in 1072, notifying the transfer of the seat of the diocese from Dorchester-on-Thames to Lincoln. Then there are boxes and boxes of charters recording gifts of property – manors, churches, lands, houses and rents – for the endowment of the chapter, the prebends and chantries of the medieval foundation. The benefactors range from great lords like Roger de Mowbray, granting the church of Empingham in Rutland to form a prebend, down to a peasant freeholder giving two acres of land in Ingoldmells to the common fund.

From the early 14th century we can see the cathedral's sophisticated administration in action through the medium of the chapter act books. We can eavesdrop on the regular Saturday meetings in the chapter house, when the residentiary canons would assemble to hear and approve the terms of a lease, to grant probate of the will of a deceased chapter clerk or to admit a new chantry priest. We might stumble across an informal meeting, as when the precentor and the archdeacon, in parley after Compline, gave orders for the induction of a vicar of the prebendal church of Corringham, 'the dean being out of town and the chancellor in his house sick'.

There also survives a magnificent series of account books. We can look over the shoulder of a 17th-century clerk of the fabric as he enters the receipt of £2 for the rent of the 'White Hart Inne' or notes down items of expenditure, for riding over to Bardney to view timber, for the carriage of lead 'up the hill', for the hire of horses to draw two loads of stone from Ancaster or for the purchase of six yards of cloth 'for the Lord Bishopp's seat'.

Other records survive in plenty, despite occasional periods of neglect – in 1609 a priest vicar had a flourishing dovecote in the muniment room, and a 19th-century visitor reported 'papers black with age, shrivelled parchments … incredibly filthy and neglected'. Nevertheless, there are multitudinous leases for properties all over the ancient diocese. There are visitation records and court books resulting from the chapter's jurisdiction over its own lands, where, for example, we can follow the provost of the common on his annual tour, travelling from village to village and hearing cases of defamation, non-payment of tithes, fornication and adultery.

If a cathedral's archives have a drawback, it is that they inevitably record the times when things have gone wrong – a chorister calling a priest vicar 'bald pate', a lay vicar striking the dean's servant with a crabtree cudgel, or the sad tale of Parson Dymoke who, coming from the Angel Inn 'in liquor', stumbled into the Chequer well and was drowned. Against these must be set the unrecorded lives of all those who, through the generations, have served the cathedral quietly, faithfully and well.

Dr Nicholas Bennett, Lay Canon, the Librarian, with one of the 260 medieval manuscripts in the cathedral library.

When the contents of the medieval library were next listed in 1668 the lecterns were filled to capacity, with the medieval manuscripts jostling for space with more than 900 printed books. Theological treatises stood next to legal commentaries; Greek and Latin classics shared space with histories and medical works. The great majority of these books remain in the collection today, but their fate might have been very different. During the confusion and upheaval of the civil wars in the 17th century, with the fighting on at least one occasion shattering the scholarly peace of the medieval library, the printed books were seized and carried off. Some said that this was done to keep them safe; others protested that it was plunder. Nevertheless, when Charles II returned to claim his throne in 1660 and a new dean and chapter came to survey the wreck of their cathedral, the oak lecterns of the library were bare of all save the medieval manuscripts, still fastened securely by their chains. ➤ p.118

Above: 'A Whale mistaken for an Island', from Conrad Gesner, Historiae Animalium, *1551.*

Left: illuminated initial from Commentary on the Epistles, *given by Treasurer Jordan* c.*1150.*

MICHAEL HONYWOOD

It was Dean Michael Honywood, more than anyone else, who brought Lincoln Cathedral back to life after the damage and neglect that had resulted from the civil wars of the 17th century. The dean and chapter had been abolished by Parliament in 1643 and its endowments confiscated and sold off. During the ensuing 17 years no maintenance or repair work was carried out on the building, the choir and organ were silenced, and many of the books in the library dispersed. When Charles II was restored in May 1660 Lincoln, along with all the other English cathedrals, was in a precarious state.

A Londoner by birth, Michael Honywood (1596–1681) spent much of his youth and early adult life at Cambridge, where he was first an undergraduate and then Fellow of Christ's College. Among his contemporaries in the college was the poet John Milton. Honywood contributed to the collection of verses lamenting the untimely death by drowning of another Christ's man, Edward King, a publication now notable for the first printing of *Lycidas*. He organized the construction of the new Fellows' Buildings at Christ's, not only raising funds but giving money himself.

Refusing to take the oath imposed by Parliament in 1643 on Cambridge dons, Honywood left the country, crossing to the Netherlands where he settled in Utrecht. He was active in the circle of Royalist exiles in Holland and fulfilled an important role by loaning books from his extensive collection to other English scholars who were pursuing research, writing tracts or seeking to understand the catastrophe that had overtaken them all. Honywood had been able to take some of his Cambridge books abroad with him, but while in the Netherlands he added considerably to his library. He was a regular visitor to the bookshop kept in The Hague by Samuel Browne, a Royalist printer whose London press had been closed down by Parliament. The notebook in which Honywood kept meticulous records of his purchases and loans of books during his exile survives in the library today, showing a range of interests that extended well beyond theology to politics, science, mathematics, travel, antiquities and linguistics. Surviving ephemera cast light on his experiences in exile: university lecture lists, book catalogues and a description of the plants in the Botanic Garden at Leiden.

News of Charles II's Restoration in 1660 was greeted with rejoicing by the exiled community in the Netherlands. On his return to England, Honywood was rewarded for his loyalty by a royal grant of the position of dean of Lincoln. Here he was able to deploy his administrative skills to good advantage, embarking on the repair of the fabric, the beautification of the furnishings and the restoration of choir and organ. He searched the archives to make sure that the cathedral endowments were restored in their entirety. In all of this his constant aim was, as he wrote, 'to see this Church in good condition, and God's service performed with due

Michael Honywood: portrait by Cornelis Jansen, in the Wren library.

decency and devotion'. Not all went smoothly. A lawsuit had to be brought against the Clerk of Works for peculation, and the organist, Dr Mudd, was often drunk and on one occasion 'fell to singing aloud' during the sermon. Honywood helped to steer the chapter through the lawsuit and produced a 'more civill' organist in Andrew Hecht, whom he may have known in the days of his exile.

Honywood's greatest gift to Lincoln was the magnificent Wren library. On his arrival at the cathedral he had discovered the medieval library denuded of a collection of some 900 printed books, which amid the confusion of the civil wars had been moved – whether for safe-keeping or from motives of plunder – down to the Lincoln School, housed in the former Greyfriars on Broadgate. He confronted the city council and secured the books' return to the cathedral, three cart-loads of learning toiling up the hill in the autumn of 1662. He initiated a new catalogue, completed in 1668. But his engagement with the cathedral's library did not end there. In 1674 he commissioned Sir Christopher Wren to design a new library building. Books and book-collecting had always been his dominant passion, and by the end of his life, he had amassed a collection of some 5,000 volumes, printed and manuscript, covering a wide range of learning and in many different languages, both classical and modern. He lived to see the new building finished and his books arranged on its shelves. He died in September 1681, bequeathing all his books to the dean and chapter, a written heritage for future generations to study and enjoy.

Marginal decoration from The Epistles of St Jerome *(Rome, 1468), the earliest printed book in the cathedral library.*

The Wren library.

Far right: letter in Sir Christopher Wren's own hand, with his signature at the bottom, setting out the rates for gilding and painting the new library in 1676.

A life-long bibliophile, Dean Michael Honywood, came to the rescue of the cathedral's library. He traced the missing books to Lincoln School, then situated in the old Greyfriars building in Broadgate. He interviewed the City Fathers, who at first shuffled, pleading ignorance ('some books from which library is conceaved by them to be in our custody'), but finally gave in to his persistent questioning. The cathedral accounts for 1662 record the payment of 4s 6d, 'for fetching 3 loade of Books from the Schoolhouse below the hill'. It was these volumes that were put in order and catalogued in 1668. Honywood, however, had only just started.

The dean himself had amassed a personal library of some 5,000 volumes. Like all great collectors he wanted to ensure that his books would remain together after his death, and to achieve this he not only bequeathed them to the dean and chapter but also determined to provide a magnificent new building to house them. To this end he turned in 1674 to Sir Christopher Wren, who had just been commissioned to rebuild St Paul's Cathedral, ➤ p.127

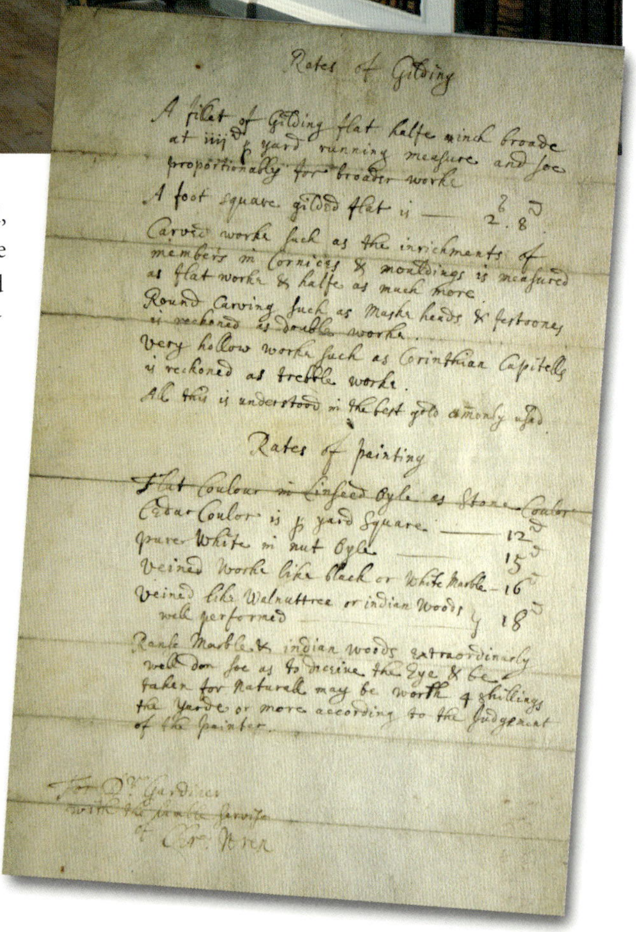

Rates of Gilding

A filet of Gilding flat halfe an inch broade at iiij^d p yard running measure and soe proportionably for broader worke

A foot square gilded flat is — 2^s. 8^d

Carved worke such as the inrichments of members in Cornices & mouldings is measured as flat worke & halfe as much more.

Round Carving such as Maske heads & festoones is reckoned as double worke.

Very hollow worke such as Corinthian Capitells is reckoned as treble worke.

All this is understood in the best gold comonly used.

Rates of painting

~~Flat Coulour in Linseed Oyle as Stone Coulor~~

Cedar Coulor is p yard Square — 12^d

Purer White in nut Oyle — 15^d

Veined Worke like black or White Marble — 16^d

Veined like Walnuttree or indian Woods well performed — 18^d

Rare Marble & indian woods extraordinarily well don soe as to deceive the Eye & be taken for Naturall may be worth 4 shillings the Yarde or more according to the Judgment of the painter.

For Dr Gardiner [illegible] [illegible] [illegible]
Chr. Wren

Opposite: 'O Lord, in thy wrath': King David prays to the Lord. From a manuscript Book of Hours (French, 15th century).

Domine ne in
furore tuo argu
as me neq; in

THE TREASURES OF THE CATHEDRAL

It is said that when the martyr St Laurence was ordered by the Roman authorities to produce for them the treasures of the Church, he gathered together all the poor, sick, blind or lame people and brought them before the prefect saying, 'See! These are the treasures of the Church'. There has always been a tension in the Church between the scriptural injunction that we should lay not up for ourselves treasures on earth and, on the other hand, the natural desire of individual believers to adorn God's house and His worship with beautiful and costly gifts. Lincoln Cathedral has been no exception to this desire. One particular focus of its expression may be found in the treasury, opened in 1960 to display rare items of gold and silver plate from both cathedral and diocese, the first such permanent exhibition in any English cathedral. Elsewhere, the cathedral houses a wealth of hidden gems, and the following sample of its treasures merely touches the surface.

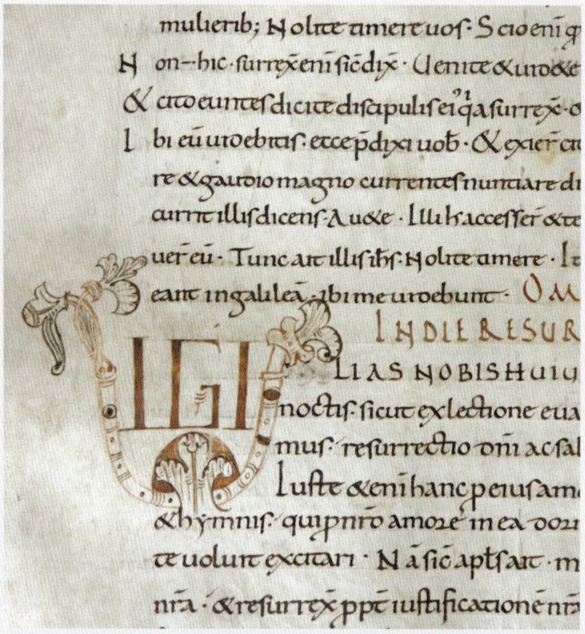

Bede, Homilies *(late 10th century): the oldest book in the cathedral library.*

THE HOMILIES OF THE VENERABLE BEDE, *c.*990

This is by a long way the oldest treasure belonging to the cathedral. A manuscript volume of 197 parchment folios, it dates from the last years of the 10th century, perhaps a hundred years before the consecration of Remigius' first building. Copied at the abbey of Abingdon, it is one of the fruits of the monastic revival led by St Ethelwold (d.984), following the anarchy of the Danish invasion, and the elegant Anglo-Caroline hand in which it is written reflects continental influences. It is probable that this manuscript belonged to the pre-Conquest cathedral at Dorchester-on-Thames, and that it was brought by Remigius to Lincoln, where it formed the nucleus of the library of the new foundation.

WRIT OF KING WILLIAM I, 1072

The oldest item in the cathedral archives, this tiny strip of parchment is an extremely rare example of a letter sent out from the court of William the Conqueror. It is addressed to Thorald, the sheriff of Lincolnshire, and to the sheriffs

Writ of William I moving the cathedral from Dorchester to Lincoln, 1072.

The Chapter Bible, c. 1100.

of all the other counties in the diocese, notifying them that the king has transferred the see of Dorchester to the city of Lincoln. It also declares that the king has given land in the city for the building of the mother church of the whole diocese, and as such it represents the foundation charter of Lincoln Cathedral. Other lands and churches given or confirmed by the king in this charter, including Sleaford, Caistor, Buckingham and Aylesbury, remained in the possession of bishop or chapter for centuries to come.

THE CHAPTER BIBLE, *c.*1100

Lincoln Cathedral's Chapter Bible has international significance as the earliest English illustrated Bible of the Romanesque period. Probably copied in the Lincoln area at the end of the 11th century, it was commissioned by Nicholas, archdeacon of Huntingdon, who bequeathed it to the library on his death *c.*1110. The characteristic Lincoln style of illustration – foliage, beasts and human figures with outsize hands and feet – shows that the manuscript was made locally. In addition to the scriptural text, it contains some unique details of the early cathedral chapter, including an inventory of the books in the library, a calendar of the anniversaries on which members of the foundation would be remembered and a list of the Psalms to be said daily by the canons.

THE SILVER SEAL MATRIX, *c.*1150

Official and legal documents issued by the cathedral body would be authenticated not by a signature but by affixing the chapter seal. A seal impressed from this matrix was attached to a charter datable to the 1150s, and like most ecclesiastical seals it is oval in shape. The matrix shows the Virgin seated, with the Child on her lap; his hand is raised in blessing. In her left hand she holds a flowering rod, an allusion to the Tree of Jesse, symbolism that is also found in the Romanesque sculpture of the cathedral and on the Tournai marble slab in the nave, thought to be from the tomb of Bishop Alexander (d.1148). On the reverse of the matrix (now covered by a plate) is an image of Christ seated on a rainbow, another theme found in the sculptural fragments of the period.

The silver Seal Matrix of the Dean and Chapter, c.1150.

THE SEAL OF ST HUGH

Tangible links with Hugh of Avalon, the saint who inspired the rebuilding of the cathedral in 1192 and in whose honour the Angel Choir was constructed, are few. This seal is a rare survival, the finest example among the only five

specimens known to exist. It is attached to a charter (dated 1189–1193) confirming the convent of Sempringham (founded by the other great saint of the diocese, Gilbert) in the possession of half of the church of Kirkby Underwood. Hugh's biographer, Adam of Eynsham, tells us that he was scrupulous in the use of his seal, ensuring that only the truth should be so attested. The image shows the bishop vested in alb and chasuble and wearing a mitre. He holds his pastoral staff in his left hand and his right hand is raised in blessing. The seal is pictured on p.84.

PATEN OF ROBERT GROSSETESTE, *c*.1253

The statutes issued by Bishop Robert Grosseteste for Lincoln diocese in 1237 emphasized the reverent use of the sacraments and the veneration of the Eucharist. The paten and chalice (pictured p.82) found in his grave in 1780 symbolize the importance of the mass in the medieval Church. They are made of silver, partly gilded, and in the central quatrefoil depression of the paten can be seen, uniquely, the figure of a bishop, vested, his right hand raised in blessing and his left hand holding a crosier. With them remain Grosseteste's episcopal ring and part of a crosier. They can be seen in the treasury along with similar groups from the tombs of Bishop Richard Gravesend (d.1279) and Bishop Oliver Sutton (d.1299). The survival of such fine grave goods of this date is very unusual.

The Lincoln Caxton, 1483.

Far left: sketches in the Thornton manuscript, c.1430.

THE THORNTON MANUSCRIPT, *c*.1430

A modest bound volume of 322 paper leaves, this is undoubtedly the most significant manuscript in the cathedral's library. The whole book was written by one hand, that of the owner. Robert Thornton, lord of the manor of East Newton in North Yorkshire, appears to have copied verse romances into the book for the instruction and entertainment of his family. He was especially interested in Arthurian stories, and the manuscript contains the only surviving copies of *Sir Perceval* and the *Morte Arthure*. The latter text provides the source from which all later versions, from Malory to Tennyson, have sprung. As well as its literary interest, the volume contains a rare collection of the works of Richard Rolle, the 14th-century Yorkshire mystic. This unique treasure house represents one of the most important witnesses to the literature of medieval England.

THE LINCOLN CAXTON, 1483

William Caxton was a successful mercer and governor of the English House in Bruges. In the course of his travels, he came across the new craft of printing, invented by Johann Gutenberg of Mainz in 1455. He went to Cologne, where he learned to print, and embarked on an English translation of *The History of Troy*. This appeared in 1474, the first book to be printed in English. Two years later Caxton moved back

William Byrd, Cantiones Sacrae, *1591.*

to London where he established a printing press close to Westminster Abbey. This book, the *Golden Legend*, is an English version of a standard collection of saints' lives. Many of the familiar stories of the saints are included, among them St Katherine and her wheel. Caxton added material of his own, including accounts of English saints. Illustrated with woodcuts, the book was printed in 1483 and proved so popular that it was reprinted at least eight times by 1527.

WILLIAM BYRD PARTBOOKS

Music is certainly one of the treasures of Lincoln Cathedral, and this rare set of five partbooks includes much of the vocal music of William Byrd, one of the greatest and most celebrated composers of his age. Appointed organist and master of the choristers at Lincoln Cathedral when in his early 20s, Byrd soon demonstrated his remarkable prowess both as performer and composer. His musical talents were not always appreciated by the increasingly Puritan chapter, and in 1572 he returned to London as a Gentleman of the Chapel Royal. He remained in the favour of Queen Elizabeth, who granted him the exclusive right to print music. These volumes include many of his most famous collections, such as *Psalmes, Sonets & Songs of Sadnes and Pietie*, *Songs of Sundrie Natures*, the *Cantiones Sacrae* and the *Gradualia*, printed between 1588 and 1611.

THE MANNERS-SUTTON COPE

The cope worn by the dean on great ceremonial occasions in the life of Lincoln Cathedral was bequeathed to the chapter by the Revd William Manners-Sutton in 1900. Made of cloth of gold, it is decorated with images of saints in gold, white, blue and grey against a red background. It is thought to have been designed by the Victorian artist Charles Kempe (better known for his stained glass) and to have been worked by the Sisters of Mercy at Clewer in Berkshire. Mr Manners-Sutton is not known to have had any connection with Lincoln, but he would have been well aware of the work of Dean William Butler in restoring the liturgical and spiritual life of the cathedral.

Detail of the Manners-Sutton cope.

EDUCATION AT THE CATHEDRAL

The cathedral continues its mission of education with the annual Church Schools Festival.

Education has always been a key responsibility of the cathedral. A medieval bishop needed to provide training for the young clerks in his household, and by the 11th century this was the task of a senior priest, often known as the *magister scholarum* (master of the schools). At Lincoln, in the chapter established by Remigius, this office was filled by Master Albinus of Anjou. One of his pupils was the future historian, Henry of Huntingdon, whose recollections of his early days in the bishop's household suggest that it included men of some intellectual standing.

Around 1148 the educational work of the cathedral was placed in the hands of a new dignitary, the chancellor, whose responsibilities included the library as well as the schools. Although no English cathedral school developed into a university, as happened in France, it is thought that Lincoln came close to doing so. The presence in 12th-century Lincoln of scholars such as Thorlak from Iceland and Gerald of Wales, together with an outstanding teacher in William de Montibus (chancellor from 1194 to 1213) reflects the esteem in which the schools were held. As late as the episcopate of Hugh of Wells (1209–35) clergy who were found to be inadequately educated were ordered to attend the cathedral school at Lincoln.

With the growth of the universities of Oxford and Cambridge, however, cathedral schools adapted their role to the teaching of grammar. At Lincoln the schoolmaster continued to be appointed by the chancellor, while the school itself, situated below the hill, was financed by an often uneasy partnership between cathedral and city. Among the young scholars were the choristers, whose education was always liable to interruption by the liturgical requirements of the cathedral. Their schoolmasters included men of distinction: William Wheatley (1316), whose commentary on Boethius still survives; John Bracebridge (1406–20), collector of more

The four institutions that are partners in the new School of Theology: the diocese of Lincoln, Bishop Grosseteste College, the University of Lincoln and Lincoln Cathedral.

DIOCESE OF LINCOLN
THE CHURCH OF ENGLAND

BISHOP GROSSETESTE UNIVERSITY COLLEGE LINCOLN

UNIVERSITY OF LINCOLN

LINCOLN CATHEDRAL

Artist's reconstruction of the medieval library of 1422, before its reduction in size in the 18th century.

than a hundred books on theology, history, medicine and grammar; William Temple (1584), later secretary to Sir Philip Sidney; and John Clarke (1622–41), whose often-reprinted textbook *Formulae Oratoriae* was used in schools as far afield as the American colonies.

It was Christopher Wordsworth, bishop of Lincoln from 1869 to 1885, who restored the prominence of education in the life of the cathedral by inviting Edward White Benson to become chancellor, with the task of establishing a theological college. Opened in 1873, the college, under the leadership of a series of outstanding wardens, provided a highly regarded course of instruction for those seeking ordination. It closed in 1996. The Lincoln School of Theology now occupies the former theological college buildings in Lincoln. A partnership between cathedral and diocese, the University of Lincoln and Bishop Grosseteste University College, the school seeks to provide the highest standards of theological study. At the same time, the cathedral itself provides a rich educational resource, through its library and through the opportunities it offers to students both young and old to deepen their understanding of the faith through an engagement with a living Christian community.

SOURCES

'The nave of the cathedral was used as a market. Straw would have been spread on the floor and animals brought in to be sold.' This piece of 'oral history' of Lincoln Cathedral can still be heard today. It does not matter that there is no evidence that it ever happened or that the use of the nave as a prestigious burial place for bishops and canons makes it extremely unlikely that it was ever used for the sale of livestock. The anecdote has been handed down from one storyteller to another, and so it must be right.

How do we know what we know about the cathedral? Oral testimony can be valuable. The memories of one old lady who saw the nave pulpit in its former home in Rotterdam before the First World War add an exciting new dimension to what we know from other sources. Such reminiscences, however, must always be tested against other evidence. Printed books about the cathedral can tell us a great deal, but writers make mistakes or they repeat the mistakes of others. It is often said that the last treasurer of Lincoln Cathedral, Henry Litherland, threw down his keys of office as the building was despoiled by Henry VIII's commissioners in 1540, saying: 'Now there are no treasures, there is no need of a treasurer.' He might well have done so, had he not been executed for treason two years earlier. The story can be traced back through reputable historians to the 18th century. It is still wrong.

The fabric of the building and its archaeology can tell us much. The archives of the cathedral, compiled objectively for practical reasons of business, can tell us more. Other contemporary documents, such as wills, letters and diaries, provide further evidence. All our statements about the history of Lincoln Cathedral must be measured against these sources, so that others who come after us can trace the reasons for what we say.

Part of the extensive library of printed books.

Researching in the cathedral's manuscripts.

destroyed in the fire of London. Wren's plans do not survive, but his work was the basis of the contract that the chapter agreed with a local builder, William Evison, to construct the new library in accordance with Wren's plans and a model supplied by Mr Thompson, one of Wren's masons.

The new building was completed in just two years. Wren's close involvement with the execution of the project is shown by a letter, preserved in the archives, setting out the rates of pay for gilding and painting, one of the last stages of the work before the books could be placed on the shelves. A small doorway at the west end of the new library gave Honywood a private entrance from the adjacent deanery. The resulting room is a masterpiece of the English baroque style, the alternately advancing and receding bookshelves along the north wall mirrored by the large south-facing windows opposite. Honywood's portrait, painted in the 1650s by Cornelis Janson, looks down the room, reflecting the pleasure he must have felt to see his collection so magnificently housed.

The dean's bequest transformed the library into a scholarly resource of considerable importance, one of the many ways in which Honywood and his contemporaries were endeavouring to restore the fortunes of the Anglican Church in the Restoration period. Its subject range was, and is, vast: the classics and antiquities of the Graeco-Roman world are joined by chronicles of the more recent past, works of literature both English (such as *Paradise Lost* by Honywood's Cambridge contemporary John Milton) and foreign (a first edition of *Don Quixote*). Scientific and medical works, for example Harvey's treatise on the circulation of the blood, can be found alongside such books of discovery as Hakluyt's *Voyages* and a magnificent series of atlases beginning with Ortelius' *Theatrum Orbis Terrarum* of 1584. The changing fortunes of the times through which the dean lived are reflected in an extensive series of pamphlets and tracts charting some of the turbulent politics of the day.

The rich variety of the library's collection of early printed books can be sampled by visiting the annual summer exhibition. Appropriate works are displayed for events, including lectures by distinguished speakers and concerts of early music, for which the acoustic of the room is ideal. The library continues to fulfil its traditional role of supporting the educational mission of the cathedral, welcoming all who are engaged in life-long learning, among them children participating in workshops, college students tackling projects, postgraduates carrying out research for their dissertations and academics from around the world in pursuit of rare editions or manuscripts. At the same time, staff and volunteers are busy behind the scenes, cataloguing, classifying and conserving this remarkable written heritage, making it accessible for the present generation while preserving it carefully for generations to come.

Conservation of the rare books.

THE GALILEE PORCH

BY PHILIP BUCKLER

Returning to the southwest transept and past the statue of Bishop Edward King, visitors will find a door leading out of the cathedral on the south side into a porch known as 'Galilee'. Amid all the comings and goings at the cathedral, the Galilee Porch has played a variety of roles. It stands self-contained in its splendour, attached to the southwest corner of the southwest transept. It boasts tall Perpendicular arches and windows and has an interior richly covered in dog-tooth carvings. One writer, Francis Bond, counted the ornament repeated 5,355 times. Others have been more modest at 4,750 examples. Visitors with good eyesight and plenty of time to spare may care to make their own assessment.

Looking up from the Galilee Porch.

The origins and purpose of such a fine entrance are somewhat obscure. It is supposed by many to have been the ceremonial point of entry for the bishop when coming into his cathedral. This is supported by the fact that directly opposite it on the south side may be found the ruins of the old medieval bishop's palace. This site was bought by Bishop Alexander after the burning of the Norman cathedral in which his house was incorporated in the West Front. He moved temporarily to lodge in the East Gate while beginning his new palace. This was enlarged by successors, such as St Hugh, and it is likely that the Galilee Porch was instigated by Bishop Grosseteste for a suitably grand entrance. The bishop would then have entered through this splendid porch (described by Pevsner as gratuitously large) into the transept alongside the Bishop's Eye window. This would have echoed the somewhat more modest entrance for the dean on the north side, known as the Dean's Door, beneath the Dean's Eye window.

The name Galilee given to such a porch suggests a variety of origins, and scholars remain divided on its meaning. Some interpret it as a place of beginnings – for it was from Galilee that Jesus set out towards Jerusalem and his passion and death. Thus a point of entry to the cathedral suggests setting out liturgically, embarking on the journey of faith in the footsteps of Jesus. Others point to Galilee as the place of commissioning for the disciples from their Risen Lord. Thus it can be seen as a point of departure – going out into the world emboldened in the faith of the Risen Christ.

Dating from 1240–50, the porch has seen many different uses over the ages. As well as a place of stately entrance in liturgy, it may well have provided a setting for market stalls in the Middle Ages. Traditionally, such areas have been the gathering place for penitents to wait before being admitted to the body of the Church. It may also have been the place where corpses were laid out before burial. In cathedrals of

Opposite: detail of the dog-tooth carvings.

Children taking part in the annual Church Schools Festival display their work.

THE CATHEDRAL'S MISSION

Every cathedral is built to the glory of God and to bear witness to his love for his world. Lincoln Cathedral is more prominent than most in standing high above the city and being visible for miles around. Its very setting is a reminder to all of God's presence in his world today, and its very architecture is a reminder of how God's love was seen pre-eminently expressed in the cross of Christ – the shape of the building itself. Thus the fabric of the cathedral speaks eloquently and in detailed description through its decoration of the story of creation, redemption and salvation. Within stone, glass and wood (and other materials) may be found the accounts of scripture and events of history that inform us of our Christian faith across the ages.

That faith is expressed not only in the building but also in what takes place within it day by day, and the regular pattern of worship bears witness to all the cathedral stands for. It is enhanced by the music, which forms so integral a part of cathedral worship. In reaching beyond the limitation of words, the music of a cathedral inspires people for whom words may seem vain.

It is an important part of a cathedral's mission not only to maintain a strong choral tradition but also to share it with others by taking the choir to visit parishes and schools, and by inviting them in to share in the resources of a strong musical tradition that has developed over the centuries.

As a place of learning and research down the centuries, Lincoln Cathedral has played an important role in education. This, too, forms part of its mission today, not just in teaching young and old alike about the Christian faith but also in encouraging debate about issues of concern for our world. Its fine library contains much that illuminates human understanding across the centuries. The opportunity to provide a setting for lectures on a wide range of topics is a key part of our mission. The chapter house, Wren library and the cathedral itself offer settings almost unparalleled for atmosphere and wonder.

In supporting the work of the bishop and his diocese, the cathedral reaches out to embrace a wide range of people today. It is the mother church of the parishes throughout the historic county of Lincolnshire and the setting for large gatherings and events that draw the diocese together in its work. For a number of charities and other organizations seeking to help those in need it provides a setting to encourage support and develop awareness.

Large numbers of schools come to visit each year, enjoying the opportunity to share something of the meaning and history of the place and its purpose. The Church Schools Festival is a celebration spread over a number of weeks in the early summer when those in year 6 (11-year-olds) from all the church schools throughout the diocese (approximately 3,500 children) come for a day to 'their' cathedral to learn about it and begin what we hope is a lifetime's affection for, and perhaps involvement with, Lincoln Cathedral.

'To Have but not to Hold' is a theme adopted in the cathedral. The inheritance received from the past is remarkable, and it is our good fortune to have so much of beauty, worth and interest. But we are determined not to hold it all to ourselves but to share it with others. This extends beyond just the building itself, for we possess a team of craftsmen and women with skills honed over the centuries. These skills and the store of knowledge accumulated here is not something to be guarded with jealousy but rather to be shared and offered for others to learn.

But the most important treasure we have is the Good News of God's love shown in Jesus Christ. This gospel is something we must not hold to ourselves – it is for sharing – and this we do not only with those who come to visit but also by taking it out in our own lives to share with all our world.

The Galilee Porch.

a monastic foundation this would have been the place set aside for the monks to receive women who had business with them. Other Galilee porches or doors exist elsewhere, but often giving on to the cathedral at the southwestern corner of the nave.

Although to many the name Galilee brings to mind the place from which Jesus set out, or to which the disciples were sent, another suggestion has been made that its name is derived from the idea of a gallery porch – and indeed at Ely Cathedral the road alongside the porch is named Gallery. This looks to the derivation of the word gallery from Galilee – recalling its Hebrew meaning of *galil hogoyim* (district of the goys [unbelievers]). Again, this may support the idea of it being a place where those awaiting reception or return into communion and worship at the cathedral were kept.

In some Cluniac establishments a Galilee porch at the west end would have housed a chapel where masses for the dead were said frequently. Again this would tie in with the use of the porch for the laying out of corpses. But there is no evidence of the room above the porch – magnificent in decoration and well lit by the fine lancet windows – being used as a chapel. Evidence seems to suggest its use in pre-Reformation times as a court of the dean and chapter dealing with matters in and around the cathedral close. A document in the archives contains the pre-Reformation oath of the steward who undertook 'truly to minister the office of stewardship of the Galilee'. That room was later used to house the muniments of the dean and chapter, and it was there in the chapter clerk's office that Lincoln's original Magna Carta hung on the wall in the early 20th century after lying unnoticed for some centuries beforehand.

The porch has been used for storage during building work in the 20th century, and it provides also a point of entry for equipment being used for special events. Its dimensions are such that it can accommodate a large modern van – as may be seen when the Hallé Orchestra unloads its instruments for its annual concert in Lincoln Cathedral. One is tempted to rejoice in the foresight of the 13th-century builders providing for 21st-century needs.

But the porch may be seen not only as a place for coming into the cathedral but also as a place for going out from it. Perhaps the pilgrim, having entered through the Judgement Door in penitence and going to the Shrine of St Hugh, may have gone out from the cathedral through the Galilee Porch, recalling the words of the Risen Lord to the women at the tomb: 'Go and tell my brethren to go to Galilee, and there they will see me.' So this Porch can be seen on our contemporary pilgrimage as the place from which we set out to proclaim the good news of God's love revealed in the life, death and resurrection of Jesus Christ.

In these days a cathedral must always hold in tension its role as a place of hospitality and welcome for those who come as pilgrims, worshippers or visitors along with its responsibility to reach out and share its message, taking its mission to the world around it. That sense of both coming and going may be the statement of the Galilee Porch today.

So the cathedral returns its visitors to the world, inspired by their encounter with eternity in this holy place, and prepared to take something of that holiness back into the world from which they have come.

THE CATHEDRAL'S INTERNATIONAL OUTREACH

The international outreach of the cathedral is fostered by those who have come here from across the world and those who have gone from here to distant lands. Among the former are the many visitors from abroad who return to their homes with the memory and excitement of their visit to be shared with others. Among the latter are significant people from history and those who forge our links today. A recent report illustrated that more than 25 per cent of our visitors came from overseas. Some will have known of Lincoln already, while for others it may have been a surprising discovery. For all, we hope, it will have been something to encourage others to visit.

One of its earliest international links came through St Hugh, originally from Avalon. Today a close kinship remains with a French church dedicated to Hugh in Vence. Pilgrims from there are welcomed to Lincoln, and welcome us in turn when we visit there.

Among the discoverers of old who set out from Lincoln is Matthew Flinders, who mapped much of the continent of Australia. An annual service at the cathedral commemorates his work and symbolizes the link with that country today (see pp.74–5).

The large number of RAF stations that have been sited in Lincolnshire has meant that many who flew from this county during the Second World War have developed a profound affection for the cathedral. Among these would be many from Australia, Poland, and the United States (see pp.72–3).

Other pioneers who set out from Lincolnshire were among the early settlers in the New World. Lincolnshire's John Smith was the first governor of Virginia, and it was

The cathedral welcomes visitors of all nationalities and faiths.

Virginia in the early 17th century: from Willem Blaeu, Le theatre du monde, 1647 [Lincoln Cathedral Library].

A visit by Sudanese Merchant Princes in 1924. Dean Fry is in the middle, and Mr Godfrey, the Clerk of Works, on the left.

good that the cathedral played its part recently in celebrating the 400th anniversary of their arrival. Loaning Lincoln Cathedral's Magna Carta to the United States has encouraged a close bond of friendship with many across the Atlantic. First travelling there for the World Fair of 1939, it went back twice in the late 20th century. More recently it has visited not only Virginia, but also Philadelphia, California and New York. On each occasion it has drawn considerable crowds, especially of schoolchildren learning the origins of their own history. Viewing what has been described as the 'birth certificate of democracy', they have been able to place it alongside their own Declaration of Independence, Bill of Rights and American Constitution. These visits have also encouraged and stimulated serious debates on contemporary issues of justice and freedom, a very real part of the cathedral's outreach in exploration and education.

A link with India has been marked by a longstanding association with the church in Tirunelveli, and it is good to welcome visitors from there to take part in the life of the cathedral and its worship. Artists from Russia and other parts of the world have exhibited their works here. Through the crafts skills we attempt to share, the Prince's Trust has sent apprentices and students from many different continents to come and spend time in Lincoln with our Works Department. Members of that department have themselves gone abroad to take part in craft conventions, sharing the skills they have developed from their medieval predecessors.

Apprentices learn skills in the Works Department.

So the net of friends and colleagues widens year by year. The Association of Friends of Lincoln Cathedral is proud to own Friends across five continents of the world who care about, and engage with, the life of the cathedral from afar.

3 THE CATHEDRAL TODAY

THE CATHEDRAL TODAY

BY GAVIN KIRK

Lincoln Cathedral is open 365 days a year, holding a minimum of four services each day, no matter what else goes on. While the rhythm of each day is basically the same, in fact no two days are identical. This chapter describes what happens here, day in, day out, together with a taste of some of the events that happen only occasionally.

Previous page: the dean's verger and the cathedral beadle work out a seating plan.

A verger holds some of the keys needed for day to day tasks – including the key to the key cupboard.

Just before 7 am each day the duty verger arrives to open up the building and make the last-minute preparations for the morning services. He or she has the building, awesome in its size and its silence and bathed in early-morning light (sometimes in Stygian darkness), entirely to themself for about 15 minutes until the clergy begin to arrive for the first 'office' of the day. *Officium* is the Latin word for duty or responsibility, and it is the primary purpose of Lincoln (and every other) Cathedral to praise God, the regular punctuation of the day with services and prayers reminding ourselves and our visitors that time belongs to God. Cathedrals are among the very few historic buildings still used for the purpose for which they were built.

Mattins (Morning Prayer) is said at 7.30 am, normally at St Hugh's Shrine, by the four canons who serve the cathedral. They are often joined by other clergy or laypeople, and visitors are always most welcome. Towards the end of Mattins the choristers enter by way of a side door and make their way in silence to the Song School, where they have 45 minutes' rehearsal each morning before school.

At 8 am the Eucharist is celebrated in one of the 13 side chapels, each of which is used regularly. The bishop or one of the canons generally takes this service, which lasts about 30 minutes. After the service the vergers clear away and prepare the building to open to visitors. Towards the end of the Eucharist those masons, glaziers, joiners and other staff of the Works Department working on the building that day will have slipped quietly into position in order to be able to begin work at 8.30 am.

The ringing of one of the two medieval bells in St Mary's (the northwest) tower at 9 am used to signal the start of the Lady Mass until the Reformation; now it marks the beginning of visitor opening hours. Around this time our duty chaplain usually arrives: this is a priest or lay minister who is available during the day to talk to visitors, to ➤ p.140

Opposite: sunlight through the stained-glass windows paints a column in the nave.

CLERGY

The cathedral is first and foremost the seat of the bishop of Lincoln and the centre from which he exercises his ministry in the vast diocese of that name. As visitor (a sort of court of appeal should things go wrong), the bishop has from early times delegated the management of his cathedral to a group of senior priests, recently expanded to include expert laypeople.

The clergy who serve the cathedral are known as canons residentiary. Four in number, their ancient titles refer to the portfolios they hold. First after the bishop is the dean, whose title means 'head of 10' (the original number of chapter dignitaries). The dean is the chairman of the chapter (the cathedral's governing body), the senior member of the foundation and, as archpriest of the diocese, a member of the bishop's senior staff. It is his responsibility to see that the cathedral's worship and mission are duly carried out, its fabric maintained, its people cared for and its statutes observed.

Clockwise from the right: the Gospel is carried in at the Eucharist; vestry prayer before a service; the subdean blesses a family bible in the Morning chapel; the dean and his verger prepare for a service.

The precentor is responsible for the worship and music of the cathedral, overseeing the work of the musicians, vergers and servers, and arranging the participation of visiting choirs. He has charge of the cathedral diary, coordinating the many different groups and individuals who wish to use the cathedral for services, concerts, exhibitions, celebrations, plays, lectures and other activities. His title means 'first singer' and he generally takes a leading role in sung services. He is supported in this by the priest-vicars, clergy from the diocese with musical and liturgical skills. He is also the canon sacrist, responsible for the collection of silver, much of which is displayed in the cathedral treasury.

The chancellor is the canon responsible for the chapter library and its priceless collection of medieval manuscripts. He oversees the cathedral's education programme, arranges those who are to preach at the services and has traditionally been involved in a senior capacity with the work of theological education in the city and diocese. More recently the chancellorship has been combined with the leadership

of the Lincoln School of Theology, bringing the work of the cathedral into an even wider context, while the running of the cathedral's historic collection is the responsibility of the vice-chancellor.

The subdean is master of the fabric, overseeing the activities of the army of skilled craftspeople who maintain, conserve and repair the cathedral's stonework, glass, timber and lead, as well as the historic properties of Minster Yard, the cathedral close. The subdean is also canon pastor, who ministers to the needs of the cathedral congregation, and master of the Hospital of the Holy and Undivided Trinity, a charity providing residential accommodation and community life for a group of elderly gentlemen at Retford.

The suffragan bishops of Grimsby and Grantham and the archdeacons of Lincoln, Stow and Lindsey are also dignitaries of the cathedral, while working full time in the diocese, and a further 33 prebendaries and 10 lay canons make up the College of Canons, whose large number reflects the historic significance of what was one of the largest dioceses in Europe.

Clockwise from the top: the beadle rings the bell to call people to worship; Susan Scatliffe and Angie Wilson make fresh sandwiches in the Refectory; taking a break in the cloister.

answer their questions about the building or its life or to give spiritual advice. Although they may bring a book with them, it is unusual to see them reading it: they are generally engaged in conversation or prayer with a visitor.

The Consistory Court Shop at the southwest end of the nave opens at 9am to sell gifts, souvenirs or mementos of your visit. You can purchase one of the many recordings of our choir or the Father Willis organ, facsimiles of some of the grotesques that adorn the building or books about Lincoln's castle and cathedral. At 10 am the Cloister Refectory opens, serving refreshments and meals to visitors and staff alike. In the summer it is pleasant to eat and drink in the Wren cloister or looking across to Tennyson's statue on East Green, but in winter it is best to be indoors. Across the road in Minster Yard from the shop is the Cathedral Centre. Formerly the home of one of the residentiaries, it has been redeveloped as an educational outreach base, where the state-of-the-art computer suite and conference rooms are used by business consultancies, school parties and local interest groups. Here the cathedral's ministry of hospitality brings together people for all kinds of events, perhaps cultural, intellectual, interfaith, recreational or, during the Christmas market, as a 'comfort stop' and control centre.

We have an army of some 500 volunteers who support the paid staff in their care of the building and in the welcome and reception of visitors. Some of these are guides, who are available, free of charge, at set times to take people on tours of the cathedral. By arrangement we can provide guided tours in most of the major European languages, as well as one or two others. Floor tours take place each weekday at

11am, 1pm and 3pm, and roof tours at 11am (sometimes) and 2pm. On Saturdays in the summer season it is possible to climb the Great Tower at 1.30pm and 3pm. Parties of visitors often prebook their own visits at different times through the Communications Office or Education Department, and these tours are tailored by specialist guides to the interests of the participants.

We try so far as possible to keep the nave clear of furniture in order that visitors may appreciate the medieval vista as they enter. In earlier times the nave was as much a community space as it was a church, and we keep that in mind in the variety of events that take place therein. Along the north arcade of the nave is a permanent exhibition of the *Forest Stations*, an imaginative representation of the traditional Stations of the Cross by William Fairbank, which beg to be touched and pondered as you pass. Each year we play host to a variety of art exhibitions, from modernist icons to botanical paintings, from boxes that explore the properties and play of light to war sculpture from Sarajevo. Most years the chapter hosts an artist-in-residence, who spends up to two years working in the cathedral and developing their own style alongside some of the world's great art and architecture. Some of our artists have gone on to mount major exhibitions in London and elsewhere.

For three weeks each year we host a Church Schools Festival, during which some 3,500 schoolchildren come to celebrate in the cathedral, participating in a carousel of worship, learning, music and other activities and, we hope, coming to feel that this is 'their' cathedral. Each of them takes away a free pass to bring their parents back with them to visit again.

Perhaps during the morning and certainly at lunchtime there will be another celebration of the Eucharist, and prayers will be said again around midday. There is usually a constant trickle of people into the Longland Chantry to leave prayers and thanksgivings or to light candles in front of the Blessed Sacrament. You will doubtless notice people nip in and out of the Morning Chapel at the west end of the cathedral: they have come to say a quick prayer or to spend some time in meditation on their way past the cathedral. ➤ p.144

Clockwise from the top: reception desk staff welcome visitors to the cathedral; a volunteer guide leads a tour of the roof; the Lincoln Imp is a popular souvenir of a visit to the cathedral.

STAFF AND SKILLS

The skill base represented by the staff of a cathedral such as Lincoln must be as wide as any commercial operation. The vergers of the cathedral, in particular, must be multi-talented, for their duties in preparing for and managing services and events and de-rigging afterwards move from furniture-moving to split-second timing, from crowd control to managing complicated lighting and audio equipment to create the right scenic effects. They are often the first port of call in pastoral situations, ranging from inebriate travellers to the suddenly bereaved, and their varied backgrounds, from chef to bouncer, afford a wealth of experience and wisdom, which is constantly employed in the service of God and neighbour.

The staff of the Works Department, headed by the Clericus Fabricae, combine artisanal skills of great antiquity with cutting-edge technology in their care and restoration of the cathedral's historic fabric. The work of the stonemasons is arguably the most romantic, as evidenced by the bold restoration of the carvings of the Romanesque frieze on the West Front or the intricate designs of the Dean's Eye window. The glazing department routinely employs glaziers from across Europe as they clean, conserve and create the stained glass, some of it medieval and extremely noteworthy.

The work of the joiners takes them from the great timbers of the roof space, which must be seasoned for several years before they can be incorporated, to helping create the

David Wheelband, Works archivist, in the Works Department archive, where the shelving system has been in use since the early 20th century.

Clockwise from below: Roy Bentham, chapter clerk and chief executive, in the Chapter Office; head carver, Paul Ellis, working on a new capital; Jo Sharpe from the Communications office puts the post into pigeonholes outside the Canons' vestry; fourth verger Kate McLean Mair irons a fair linen cloth used for covering altars.

state-of-the-art lavatory block off the cloister, which opened in 2009 (see p.107). Our lead-workers boast never having suffered a theft from the building, which may owe as much to the scale or altitude of the cathedral roof as to anything else, and the conservators face a Herculean task in recording and preserving for posterity the fabric of this mighty building. The Domus team cares for over 70 houses in and around Minster Yard, some of them of very great age and architectural significance. We also have a thriving apprentice scheme, which makes the skills practised here available to the next generation, and we are delighted now to be welcoming apprentices from abroad.

In the Chapter Office the chapter clerk and chief executive presides over a smaller but no less dedicated and diverse team, where the exigencies of the financial, legal, administrative, property, fundraising and human resource aspects of our community life are managed. Lincoln Minster Shop consists of the refectory off the northeastern corner of the cloister with its ministry of hospitality to tourist and local, and the Consistory Court Shop at the west end of the cathedral, selling a wide variety of gifts and mementos. Across the road is the Cathedral Centre, formerly the dwelling of a canon residentiary, which welcomes groups from the cathedral, the local community and further afield within its elegant and beautifully restored walls. The centre is a meeting-point for all sorts and conditions of people, from newly-weds celebrating their reception to businesses investing in their employees by providing developmental training to workshops run by specialist interest groups in order to cultivate interest and garner support.

John Campbell, the dean's verger, in his office in one of the 13th-century chapels in the north east transept.

Below: A lunchtime service in the Angel Choir.

The stone bench along the north and south walls of the nave was built as a resting place for the old and sick during services – hence the expression 'the weakest go to the wall' – and today still provides a place for weary visitors to rest their feet.

Right: the coronation scene in The Young Victoria, *starring Emily Blunt, was filmed in the cathedral.*

The intercession cards that visitors fill in and leave at one of several points around the building are collected and are offered at one of the many services or by the cathedral's own prayer group.

Most weeks we will have a lunchtime concert, perhaps in the cathedral or more often in the chapter house, which can seat smaller numbers more conveniently. These may be anything from visiting American gospel choirs to a gamelan recital, and very often the talented youngsters of Lincoln Minster School give coursework recitals at which anyone is welcome. These concerts are always free, and the standard is usually high.

During the day you will almost always see some part of the cathedral being cleaned by Cynthia, our full-time cleaner, or one of the vergers or volunteers. This is more than a full-time occupation, but it has to be fitted around the many other uses to which the building is put. We may have a visit of a school for its founder's day celebration, a visiting High Court judge, resplendent in scarlet and ermine, coming to prayer with the high sheriff and the court service before presiding over the courts in Lincoln, a couple celebrating the golden jubilee of their marriage or two young people just beginning their life together. Or perhaps there is a flower festival going on, the building festooned in blooms arranged by over 50 flower clubs across the region, or a major art exhibition. We have even been a film set (in August 2005) for a Hollywood blockbuster, whose scenes managed to be filmed without any interruption to our daily cycle. The recent filming of the ever-popular BBC programme *The Antiques Road Show* provided enough material for not one but two episodes, with guests varying from nuns to bricklayers. ➤ p.148

Opposite: Cynthia Smith polishes the magnifying mirror which gives a startlingly clear view of the roof bosses in the retro choir.

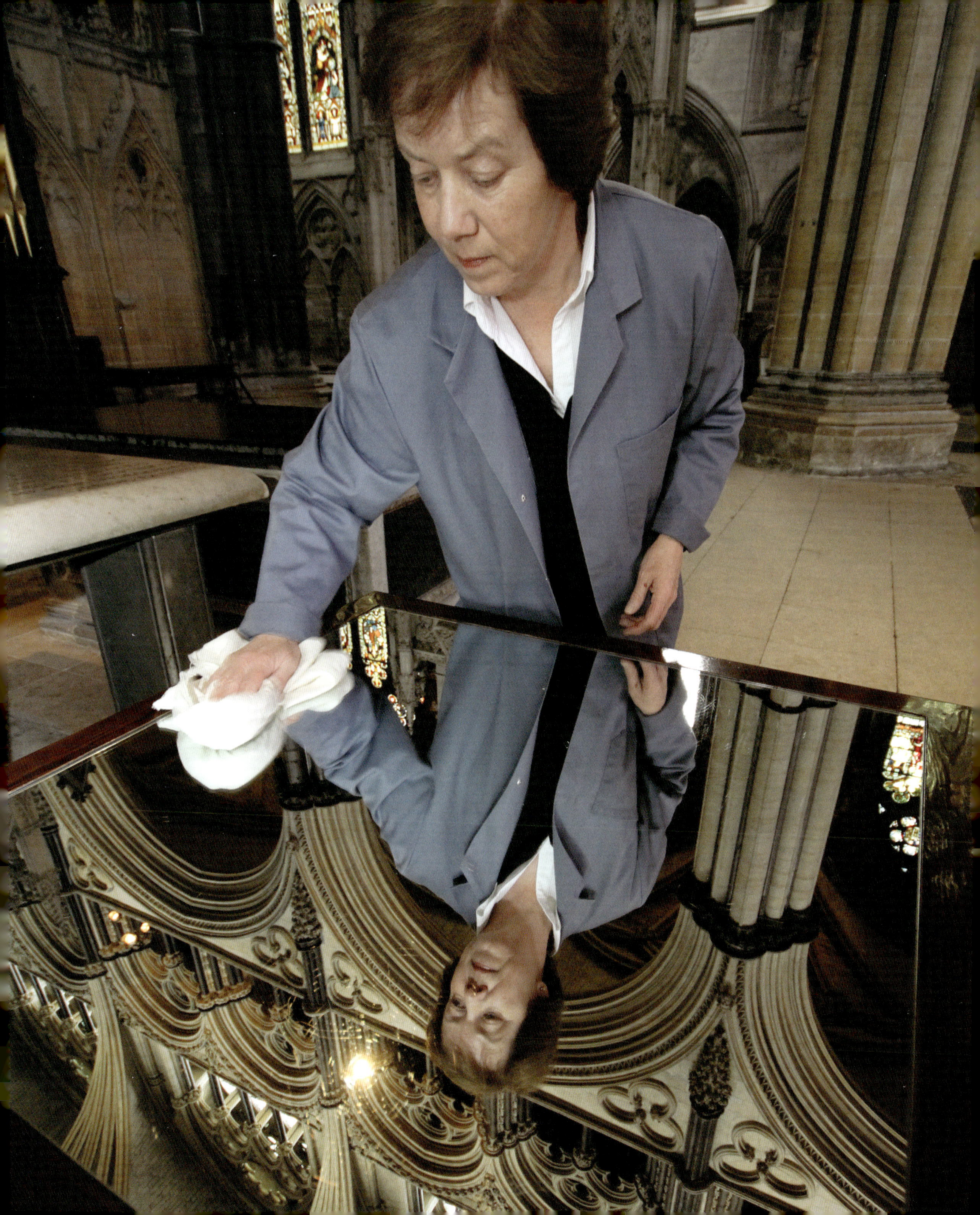

VOLUNTEERS

The cathedral's many activities are made possible by an army of about 500 volunteers. Representing almost every facet of life, they bring their skills and experience to bear in caring for the building and its treasures and interpreting them. Some have a long history, like the Company of Ringers, who date their foundation back to 1612. They ring the bells in the southwest tower for the services on Sundays and special occasions, maintaining the peculiarly English science of change-ringing. Experts in book conservation and repair work in the cathedral library under the aegis of NADFAS (National Association of Decorative and Fine Arts Societies) to maintain our historic collection of antique books, while other volunteers introduce people to Honywood's *athenaeum* and its fascinating contents and steward the lectures and concerts that take place in the Wren library. Members of the Embroidery Guild make and restore vestments and altar furnishings for the cathedral's 14 altars as well as accepting commissions from further afield, while seamstresses deal with the endless task of caring for the choir's robes as the choristers continually grow and change.

Right: Gilly Brown arranging flowers.

Jane Drummond, a member of the Embroidery Guild.

The daily round of services incorporates the contributions of professionals and volunteers alike: the altar servers of the Fellowship of St Hugh, the volunteer vergers who augment the work of the full-time department; the stewards who welcome worshippers to services and visitors to concerts and functions, maintaining order and calm throughout the building and responding to individual needs; the flower arrangers whose creativity harnesses the beauty of natural flora to the splendour of the architecture.

The building itself is interpreted by a number of different groups of guides. The largest group guide visitors round the building in both general and specialist tours and in a number of foreign languages. Twice most days those with a head for heights can follow a roof tour, exploring parts of the building not otherwise accessible, and the very hardy can follow the tower guides up the central tower, visiting the clock room, Great Tom of Lincoln, the tenor bell in the central tower and enjoying the panoramic view from the very top. Different themed trails are available, from children looking for depictions of animals to those appreciating the influence of the Jewish community over the centuries. The casual visitor may have recourse to the information desk, and the cathedral's solitary cleaner is supported by a number of dusters, sweepers and tidiers.

The chapter's various committees are largely made up of volunteers. Some are lay members of chapter itself, appointed for their skills in management, human resources, business and fundraising. Others sit on the finance and shop committees, the Preservation and Music Councils,

Paul Paynton, the fifth verger, polishing silver in the Canons' Vestry.

Left: visitors on a guided tour of the eastern roof.

the Library Advisory Committee, or the Cathedral Council, with its wide representation, reviewing and supporting the spiritual, pastoral, evangelistic, social and ecumenical work of the cathedral.

To these should be added those parochial or retired clergy and readers who regularly give up half a day or more to serve as duty chaplain, making sure that there is always a friendly face to whom visitors may speak confidentially on matters of a spiritual or personal nature.

Scene from the 2008 Mystery Plays.

Below: Martin Chambers mows the grass.

Military funeral [Courtesy of the Lincolnshire Echo*].*

Every four years a local group of enthusiasts puts on an adaptation of the *Lincoln Mysteries*, continuing the centuries-old tradition of mystery plays. Each cycle is unique, bringing together professionals and amateurs to present timeless truths in contemporary media.

At 3pm the bell rings out again, reminding us of the hour when Jesus died on the cross to save the world. After a pause, the life of the building continues. Perhaps a group will have arranged to rehearse their movements for a service the following Sunday, and there is a number of these throughout the year. Some are hardy annuals, like the civic service to inaugurate a new chairman of the county council, the Battle of Britain commemoration in September or the annual Remembrance Service on the Sunday nearest Armistice Day. On a smaller scale is the little service every March, for which the Australian High Commissioner or his deputy travels from London to celebrate with our local branch of the Britain–Australia society the life and achievements of Matthew Flinders, the Lincolnshire-born navigator and cartographer of southern Australia.

Sometimes a service will be held in the nave because the anticipated congregation is too big to hold it anywhere else in the city or county. In the same summer we held both the wedding of a Nigerian couple from a neighbouring parish who wished to invite 700 guests to celebrate with them and, only shortly afterwards, the funeral service for a bomb disposal soldier from the city who died defusing a bomb while on active service in Afghanistan. His funeral brought the city to a respectful standstill. Other services will be 'one-offs', such as the gathering to present medals to veteran Land Army girls from the Second World War or the dedication of young yew trees to be planted all over the county to celebrate the millennium.

Perhaps the cathedral will be resounding to the practice of an orchestra putting the finishing touches to tonight's concert. You may turn a corner and find a group of pilgrims, carrying candles and singing, in procession towards the shrine of St Hugh or a cluster of people praying together

in one of the side chapels. Twice or so each year you might find a 'spirituality taster day' in progress, when people are encouraged to come and explore different forms of spirituality, or a 'fresh expressions' celebration employing the latest technological and musical effects.

One of the most sustained periods of heavy use of the cathedral is the city's annual Christmas market. More than 100,000 visitors are attracted by the four-day festival, which sees 300 stalls set up in a German-style market in uphill Lincoln. Most of the visitors make their way into the cathedral, whether for mulled wine and mince pies in the chapter house, recitals by the cathedral choir, local bands, recorder groups or carol singers, retail opportunities in the Cathedral Shop, the Christmas market carol service (standing-room only) or in search of a little rest and recuperation amid all the hustle and bustle. The market is worth £10 million to Lincoln's economy, and the cathedral

The Christmas market attracts many visitors to the cathedral.

On the way to rehearsal.

Right: The canons' verger washing up after early morning communion.

is proud to play its part in supporting the city that supports it. Indeed, an independent survey commissioned recently concluded that the cathedral sustains 7 per cent of jobs in the East Midlands heritage tourism industry and supports the employment of 649 workers.

After 4.15pm either the boy choristers or the girls arrive for their second rehearsal of the day in the Song School, getting ready for Evensong later in the afternoon. After tea in the cloister refectory they move to St Hugh's Choir at 4.55pm, where they are joined by the lay vicars, the choir's singing men, hot-foot from their jobs or studies. There then follow 20 minutes of rehearsal with the organist, after which St Hugh's Choir is opened to those who wish to attend Evensong at 5.30 pm. The solemn singing of choral services in the cathedral dates back to its foundation in the 11th century, and there has been a choir school here since at least the 13th century. The service is essentially that composed by Archbishop Cranmer in the 16th century, but it contains texts and melodies that are much earlier, many of which would have been familiar to St Hugh, the rebuilder of this cathedral at the end of the 12th century. The essence of this service is praise: words, inspired by God, used to worship him and lift our minds and hearts. If you are able to attend this service, you should get a real idea of what it is to which all of our activity and care leads.

Evensong is sung six days a week as part of our daily offering, but it also forms the matrix into which many other celebrations are set. Each year the bishop appoints new members to the College of Canons, who are installed at Evensong on St Hugh's day with a congregation of hundreds. A couple may be celebrating a significant marriage anniversary with only a few family and friends to swell the regular congregation. The Knights Templar may be attending in their distinctive uniforms, or the work of a local charity might be celebrating the achievements of its volunteers. During the summer months we welcome visiting choirs from this country and abroad while our own choir is on holiday, and some of these return regularly as relationships are built up between us.

The congregation gather for worship.

Evensong finishes at about 6.15pm. In the summer months visiting continues until 8pm, but from September the building closes after Evensong unless there is a concert, service or other function in the evening. There are many concerts, and some, like the world-famous Hallé orchestra or The Sixteen, fill the nave to capacity – tickets for G4 sold out within 24 hours in 2006. Other events, perhaps by more local artists, are held in a transept, the chapter house or the Wren library. Perhaps one of the three local institutions of higher education will hold an awards ceremony for its recent graduates and their proud families, or those who have prepared for many months to become local ministers will receive their mandates from the bishop. On other occasions there might be a lecture in theology or current affairs, or a meeting to commission all the churchwardens in one area of the diocese. A recent innovation is the fundraising dinner in the nave at which we are able to seat 500 people to relax, enjoy fine food and entertaining speakers.

It might be getting on for midnight before the last paper is cleared away, the final chair straightened and the preparations made for the early-morning services of the following day. Even with the building officially closed, however, work goes on – the bell-ringers practise weekly, as do the cathedral's organists, using the stops that would prevent visitors or workers from hearing the person next to them during opening hours – and sometimes lucky groups are given a candlelit tour with the building entirely to themselves.

All of this is what happens on 'normal' weekdays. On Sundays, of course, there is worship practically continuously from 7.45am until 1pm, with Evensong slightly earlier at 3.45pm. Often there are special services on a Sunday – when the bishop holds an ordination, for example, or when we are hosting those coming to celebrate a particular event. Visitors are still welcome to look around the nave if the service is taking place in St Hugh's Choir, but if it is a nave service visiting is restricted while it is taking place. A few services and events have to be on a ticket-only basis, but we are delighted to welcome visitors or first-timers to share in our life at whatever level they find is comfortable.

This rather long descriptions gives an impression of the kaleidoscope of activity that goes to make up the life and mission of Lincoln Cathedral in the early years of the 21st century. It is a thrilling, exhausting and energizing experience to share its life for even a short period, and all those who work here in whatever capacity are conscious of the immense privilege we enjoy.

FUNDRAISING

A calculation in 2009 revealed that it cost 13p a second to run Lincoln Cathedral. That frightening statistic – very much a fluid one – is the reason that we have to spend a significant amount of time in raising extra funding. Cathedrals receive no state support, and many receive only the salaries of the dean and two canons from central Church funds. The cathedral architect has warned that for the foreseeable future £1.6 million a year must be spent simply to maintain the fabric of the building in good condition.

The cathedral's three main sources of income are investment income, rents from properties and the charges made at the entry desk. The shortfall between this and the annual costs of about £4.5 million has to come through fundraising if the cathedral is not to slip into deficit, to say nothing of ambitious projects for the future. At Lincoln we are fortunate in the determination of many people to make sure that this money is raised each year.

Keith Jones, Secretary of the Friends of Lincoln Cathedral.

The Association of Friends of Lincoln Cathedral is an international body committed to the preservation and beautification of the cathedral and its worship. Through its generosity and the hard work of its officials we are able to commission new artefacts, which could otherwise not be contemplated.

The Fabric Fund (formerly the Preservation Council) works to raise money for the maintenance and repair of the cathedral fabric, building up an endowment that allows major capital projects to be undertaken that would be impossible out of annual income. Led by the High Steward of Lincoln, H.M. Lord Lieutenant of Lincolnshire, and through a series of local committees, a variety of fundraising events are held that seek to build upon the special place the cathedral holds in the hearts of Lincolnshire people.

The Music Council is dedicated to raising an endowment that will pay for cathedral music – which currently costs about £500,000 each year – in perpetuity. This will include the costs of the salaries of the organists and choirmasters, the salaries of the lay vicars and choral scholars, the bursaries of the choristers and the upkeep of the cathedral's four organs. Events are held, all with a musical theme, that serve to widen the constituency of those who hear and appreciate the cathedral's music and to raise awareness of the contribution made by many former cathedral choristers to the musical life of the nation.

The Library Advisory Committee exists to support the work of the cathedral librarian and his staff and to provide expert advice on the care and repair of our historic collection. This is an ever-developing science, and the technology that supports it is costly.

One of the ways in which the chapter seeks to raise interest and support for the cathedral and its mission is through one of its most prized possessions – one of the four original exemplars of the Magna Carta of 1215. One of the most significant documents in the history of Europe, Magna Carta's influence can still be identified today, and through a series of carefully planned visits to the United States and Europe its key role is explored and celebrated.

This building up of communities of friends is central to our fundraising initiatives, and we are keenly aware of our responsibility to be in partnership with other institutions and groups in the regeneration of our community. In our concern to make ends meet we try not to forget the economic impact that the cathedral has on its community. Quite apart from its primary religious vocation it has recently been calculated that the cathedral contributes 7 per cent of all jobs in the tourism sector of the entire East Midlands region, and we are committed to supporting those who help to support us, including the local business community and tourism industry.

One of the ways in which many people help is by remembering the cathedral in their wills. We are fortunate in receiving a significant number of legacies each year, both large and small, whether to the general fund, to a specific project or to one of the three main fundraising organs in support of whichever area of work or mission particularly interested the donor (see p.158). Books, organ pipes or indeed stones can all be 'adopted' to creating a lasting memorial to a loved one or as an imaginative birthday of Christmas gift.

A fundraising dinner in the nave.

Left: The fundraising team, from left to right: Angie Chappell, Sally Crawford and Fiona Howick.

So far almost everything described is done by volunteers, but mention must be made of the talented and resourceful team who form the cathedral's small fundraising team. Their central work undergirds, supports and helps to administer a diverse and multi-faceted fundraising organization, which is crucial to the cathedral and its mission.

4 LOOKING TO THE FUTURE

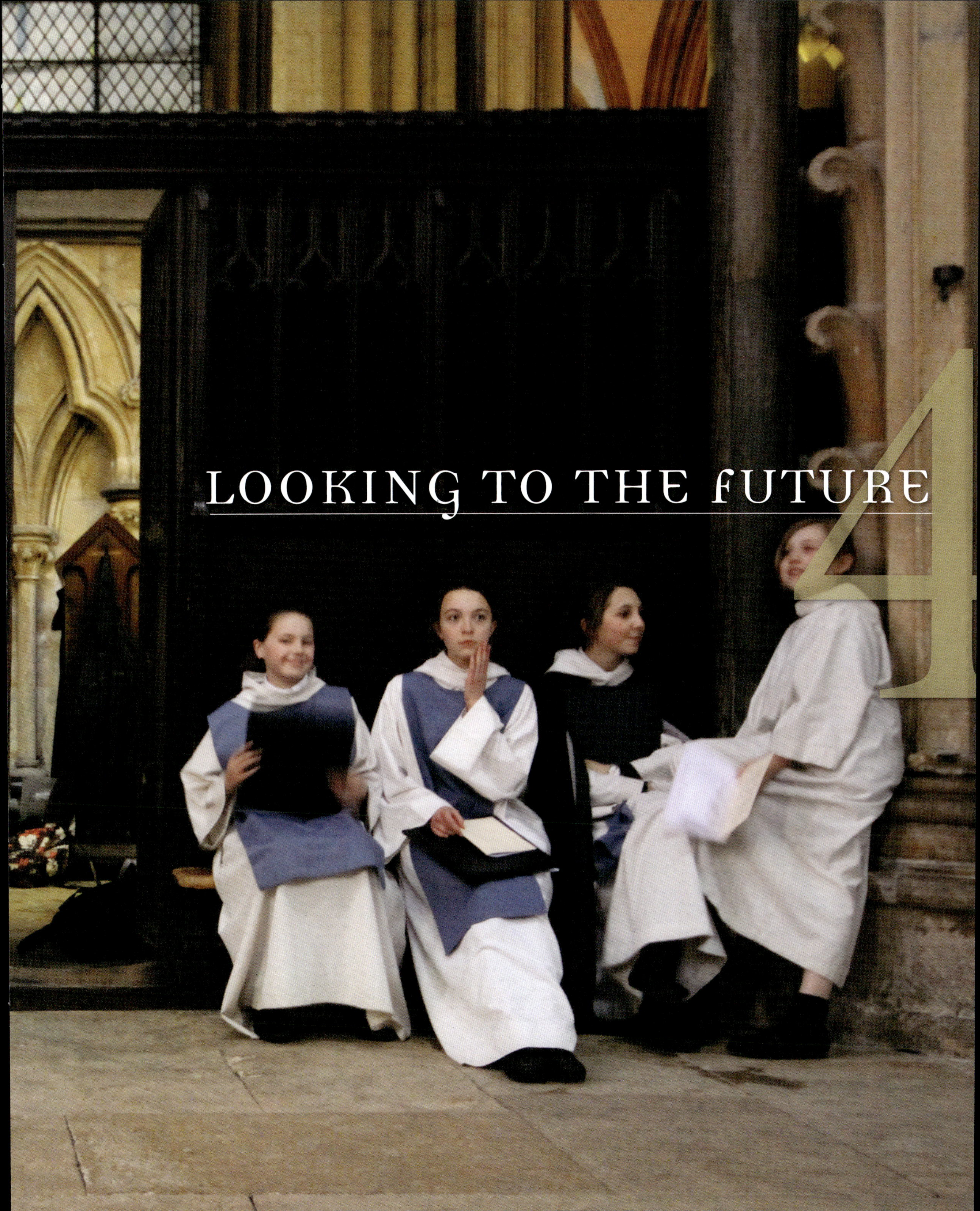

LOOKING TO THE FUTURE

BY PHILIP BUCKLER

Previous page: Burghersh chantresses waiting for worship.

HRH The Prince of Wales accompanied by Paul Atkin, Team Leader of the masons, meets Michael Graves and apprentice Glenn Miller.

A cathedral tells of the past, engages with the present, but must always be looking to the future – both in time and in eternity.

This comes as a surprise to many who see only an ancient building and are taken aback to realize how busy it is day by day. Yet they hardly imagine how forward-looking we must be. For example, young oak trees must be planted now if we are to have sufficient mature wood to replace roof timbers in years to come. Future sources of Lincolnshire limestone must be identified to provide the materials necessary to replace the fabric damaged by the harsh weather conditions on so exposed a setting. Our programme of maintenance is detailed, planning for 10, 20 and 100 years hence. The traditional skills required to look after this fine medieval building need to be handed on to young apprentices and craft workers. A fine musical tradition takes years to build up and evolves over centuries, and it, too, must ever be looking to the future to sustain and develop its potential in the children of each new generation.

It is often said that our cathedrals are the jewels in the crown of our heritage in Britain, but unlike many such remarkable buildings, cathedrals are unusual in that they are still fulfilling the purpose for which they were built. They offer people a place to discover both God and themselves. They offer society a place to express the deepest feelings of humanity, both in sorrow and in joy. They offer to all who are seeking after truth and meaning in life a place where such exploration may be carried out honestly and fearlessly. Perhaps they have never been needed so much as they are in today's world and in the times that lie ahead.

To spend time in pilgrimage to Lincoln Cathedral is to realize that every age has contributed something of itself to the living and evolving entity that is a cathedral today. It is important that we do not just hold to the past or become obsessed with the demands of the present. We must contribute things from our own time to hand on to posterity. So the need to create and commission works of art and beauty to adorn the cathedral and enhance its mission remains a priority for every dean and chapter.

Of course, the costs of maintaining such a building are enormous. With no regular state aid, cathedrals must raise their own money to fulfil their role. Visitors are generous in their support, but the sums required demand more of us all. We are aware that Lincoln Cathedral has been built and maintained by those who love it from medieval times to the present day. The people of Lincolnshire and beyond – for now we include many from all over the world – share in helping us to care for and cherish this magnificent building. This in itself is an act of worship and a tribute to all who in one way or another are the 'living stones' that make up

Opposite: Lincoln Cathedral dominates the surrounding countryside.

LEGACIES

Over the centuries people both rich and poor have left money or estates to further the work of Lincoln Cathedral. A Benefactions Book records these, and we find examples such as:

- *1235 Bishop Hugh of Wells bequeathed all the cut timber on his estates for the use of the fabric*
- *1486 Marion Gibson of Raithby by Bolingbroke, 6 d*
- *Elizabeth Falconer of Sibsey, a pair of rosary beads of jet, with three silver rings and one gold ring*
- *1681 Dean Michael Honywood: 'my library of books in whatsoever language or volume, to be kept in the library lately erected'*
- *1900 Revd William Manners-Sutton bequeathed the magnificent jewelled cope, now worn by the dean on great ceremonial occasions*
- *2010 A Lincoln lady bequeathed a residual amount of £800,000 to the cathedral's fabric fund*

In this way the people of Lincolnshire and beyond have ensured that they play their part, not only in life but also after death, to provide for the needs of the cathedral so that it may be safely handed on to continue its work in serving future generations.

This pattern of legacy giving continues today, and all it requires is a codicil in a will indicating a bequest to Lincoln Cathedral of a specific amount or a percentage of an estate. In this way people from across the world can know that they, too, are sharing in the ongoing life of this wonderful place.

Note the mug on the table in the Vergers' Vestry, where one of the vergers has been taking a break.

Lincoln Cathedral. The names of just some of those who belong in our own day may be found in the list of subscribers at the end of this book.

This is undoubtedly one of the world's greatest cathedrals. Those who are privileged to be associated with it are always keen to share its joys and wonders with others. It is a holy place for all. We are proud to have it, but not to hold it to ourselves.

As the pilgrim leaves this sacred place, so the great cathedral remains, as it has down the centuries, continuing

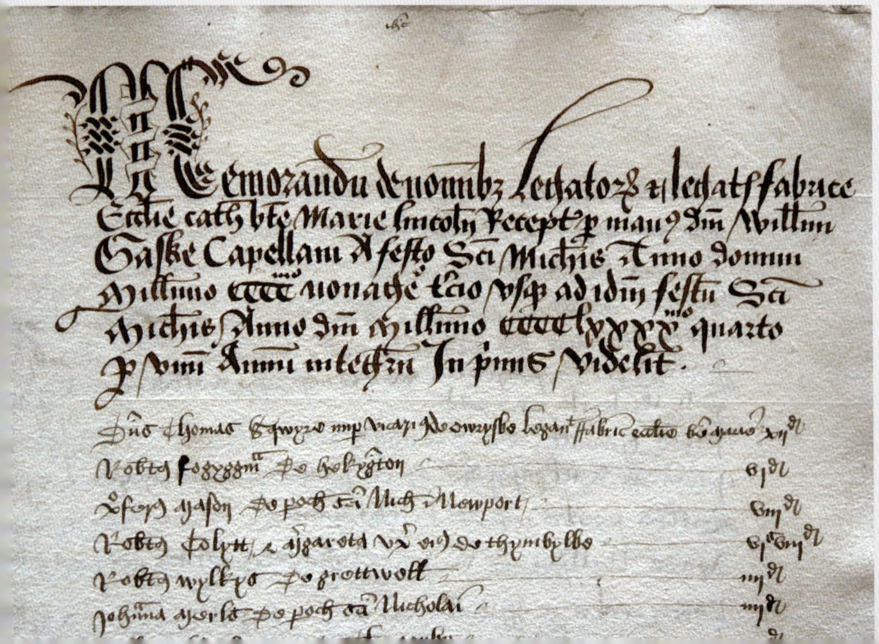
Memorandu de nominibz legatorz et legatis fabrice
Ecclie cath bte Marie lincoln Recept p manus Dni Willm
Gaske Capellam a festo Sci Michis Anno domini
Millmo cccc nonagesimo tcio usq ad idm festu Sci
Michis Anno dni Millmo cccclxxxx quarto
p unu Annu integru In pmis videlt.

Benefactions to the cathedral in 1493–94.

to pray for all who have passed through its doors and for the world in which we live. It points us to look forward to the future, with imagination, faith and an openness to change. It invites us all to be open to God and his love – the Christian gospel that has been proclaimed here down the centuries and will be throughout the ages to come.

The dean, wearing the Manners-Sutton cope, is led into the nave at the start of a special service.

Left: a child watches the procession at a Battle of Britain commemoration service.

Right: Dr John Saxbee, Bishop of Lincoln 2001–11.

TIMELINE

BY MARY LUCAS

*c.*60	Roman legionary fortress established
*c.*90	Lincoln made one of four *colonia* in England, with the name Lindum Colonia
314	The bishop of Lincoln is present at the Council of Arles; the first mention of Christianity in Lincoln
*c.*630	Paulinus builds a stone church in Lincoln
1066	William, duke of Normandy, becomes William I, the Conqueror, of England
1067	Remigius becomes the first Norman bishop in England
1068	A castle is built in the southwest corner of the Roman enclosure
1072	The see is moved to Lincoln from Dorchester-on-Thames, with Remigius as bishop
1072	The cathedral is built in the southeast corner of the Roman enclosure
1092	The cathedral is consecrated; Remigius dies
1124/41	Fire destroys the cathedral roof
1123–48	Bishop Alexander (Alexander the Magnificent) vaults the cathedral, embellishes the West Front and adds the frieze
1185	The cathedral suffers major damage in an 'earthquake' (earth tremor)
1186	Hugh of Avalon becomes bishop
*c.*1190	The Roman wall is breached to allow the cathedral's eastward extension
1192	Bishop Hugh starts to rebuild in the Gothic style
1200	Bishop Hugh dies; his grand funeral takes place in the new choir
1215	A copy of Magna Carta (still extant) is sent to the cathedral
1220	Bishop Hugh is canonized
1220	The Dean's Eye and Bishop's Eye rose windows are completed
1220–40	The rebuild is completed; the nave is widened at the west end to join on to Romanesque west block
1237	The new central tower collapses, destroying the choir screen and damaging the choir
1235–53	Bishop Grosseteste rebuilds and heightens the central tower; the city wall is breached to extend the cathedral further to the east after the demolition of the apsidal east end

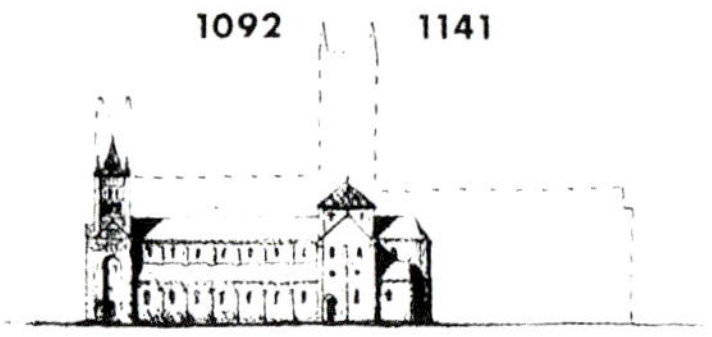

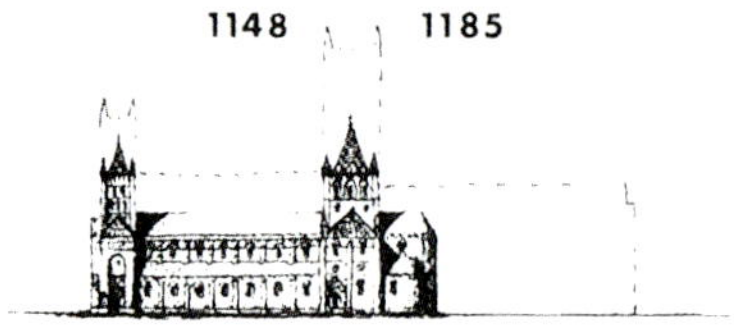

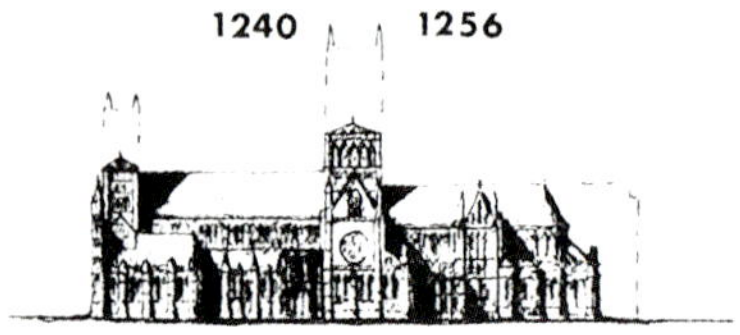

1256–80	The Angel Choir is built
1280	St Hugh's body is transported to two new shrines
1285	The cathedral and its surrounding residences are surrounded by the close wall
1297	The cloister is built
1301–27	Edward I and Edward II hold Parliaments in the chapter house
1310	Knights Templar are tried in the chapter house
1310	A cathedral organ is mentioned for the first time
1311	The cathedral becomes the world's tallest building on the completion of the new central tower with its spire
1330	The new Bishop's Eye window is built with unique tracery; a new choir screen is completed
*c.*1350	St Hugh's head shrine is built
1370s	Choir stalls and misericords are added
1350–80	The treasurer, John of Welbourne, pays for major works: the gallery of kings, a central tower vault, the great west window and tracery
1396	The marriage of Katherine Swynford to John of Gaunt takes place
1403	Katherine is buried
1420	The western towers are raised and capped with spires; a timber-framed common chamber is built
*c.*1421	The library is built on the east side of the cloister
1431	Bishop Fleming's chantry chapel is built (the first cadaver tomb)
1490	Bishop Russell's chantry chapel is built
1529	Bishop Longland's chantry chapel is built
1534	Henry VIII declares himself head of the Church in England
1536	The rebels of the Lincolnshire Rising assemble in the chapter house
1540	The destruction of cathedral shrines and images and the removal of treasures begins
1541	Henry VIII and Catherine Howard stay in the bishop's palace and order more destruction
1547	Chantries are dissolved
1548	The spire on the central tower blows down

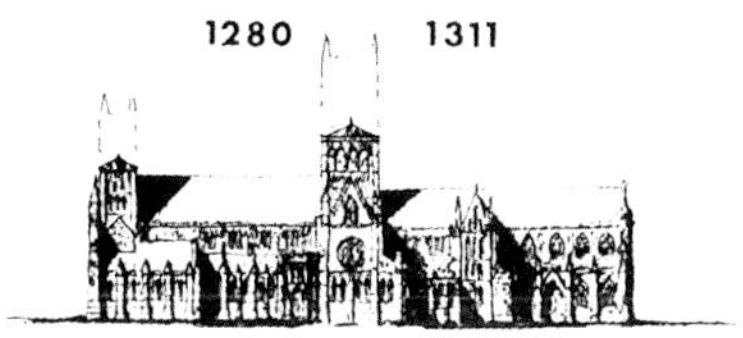

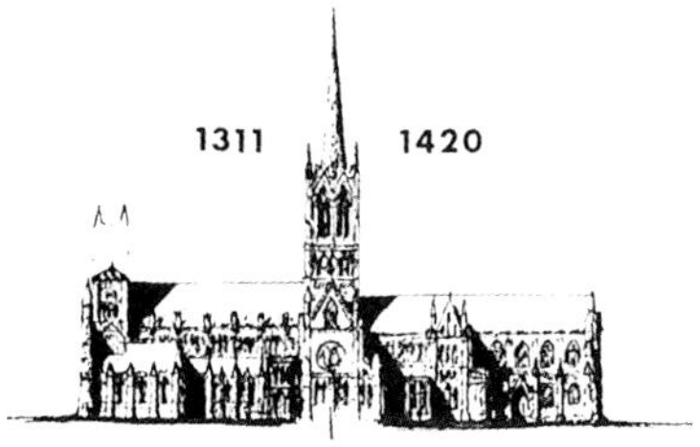

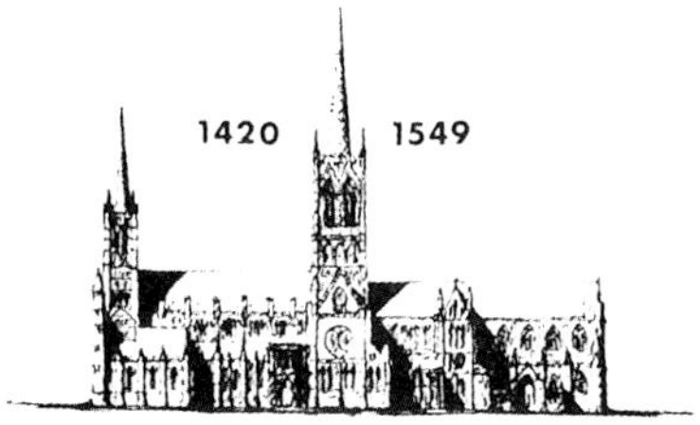

1549	The Prayer Book in English is published; services in English and clerical marriages are permitted
1612	The Company of Ringers is established, the oldest in England
1641	Fearing for their destruction, William Dugdale records all the cathedral monuments
1642	Civil war breaks out in England
1643	Royalist forces recapture Lincoln and burn the bishop's palace
1643	Cathedral chapters are abolished
1644	Cromwellian forces, who had captured Lincoln, carry out the major destruction of cathedral monuments and windows and remove cathedral treasure
1649	Charles I is executed
1660	The monarchy is restored under Charles II
1660	Cathedral chapters are re-established
1660	Michael Honywood returns from exile in Holland and becomes dean
1674	Honywood pays for a new library, designed by Wren, to house his collection of books
1660–90s	The cathedral is refurbished, including the addition of a brass lectern and candelabra
1702	The organ is re-sited on top of the choir screen
1726	The weakened West Front is strengthened by James Gibbs by the insertion of cross-walls
1775	The centre of the main wall is pierced by James Essex to restore the view down the nave
1769	The present reredos is erected behind the high altar in the choir; battlements are built on the central tower
1782	The repaving of the nave removes all traces of earlier burials
1793	A section of a Roman mosaic floor is found in the cloister; it is now under the library staircase
1807	The spires are removed from the western towers
1835	Great Tom bell is recast in London and brought to the cathedral
1852	The apse of the Romanesque cathedral is unearthed in St Hugh's Choir
1850s–60s	Most of the windows are reglazed
1860–79	The western towers are restored
1884	The 18th-century railings are removed from outside the west end; the ground is lowered

1885–1910	Bishop King, renowned for sanctity, is prosecuted for ritual offences
1913	A bronze statue of Bishop King is erected
1914	The diocesan library, the gift of Dean Wickham, is built; it is now the coffee shop
1915	The nave pulpit is presented in memory of Chancellor Edward Benson
1914–66	The services chapels are refurbished
1921	Dean Fry goes to the USA on the first fundraising mission for repairs
1932	The Duke (later George VI) and Duchess of York visit the cathedral; there is a service of thanksgiving for the completion of extensive repairs
1936	The Friends of Lincoln Cathedral is founded
1945	The bishop's residence is moved from the palace to a house in Eastgate
1956	Duncan Grant paints murals in the Russell chantry chapel
1960	The treasury is opened to public, the first of its kind in an English cathedral
1961	The cathedral school reopens (after a 42-year gap) to educate choristers
1972	The 900th anniversary of the cathedral's foundation is celebrated; floodlights are given by the city; a shop is opened in the Consistory Court
1980	Elizabeth II visits to mark the 700th anniversary of the Angel Choir
1986–2001	The restoration of the Romanesque frieze is undertaken together with the carving of new panels
1986	Sculpture is added to St Hugh's head shrine to mark the 800th anniversary of his episcopacy
2000	Elizabeth II presents Maundy Money in the cathedral
2006	The Prince of Wales visits on the completion of the restoration of the Dean's Eye rose window
2008	The new lavatory block is built
2009	Magna Carta is awarded UNESCO Memory of the World Status and exhibited again in the USA
2010	The archbishop of Canterbury, Rowan Williams, celebrates the centenary of Bishop Edward King in the cathedral

MAP OF THE CLOSE & CATHEDRAL FLOOR PLAN

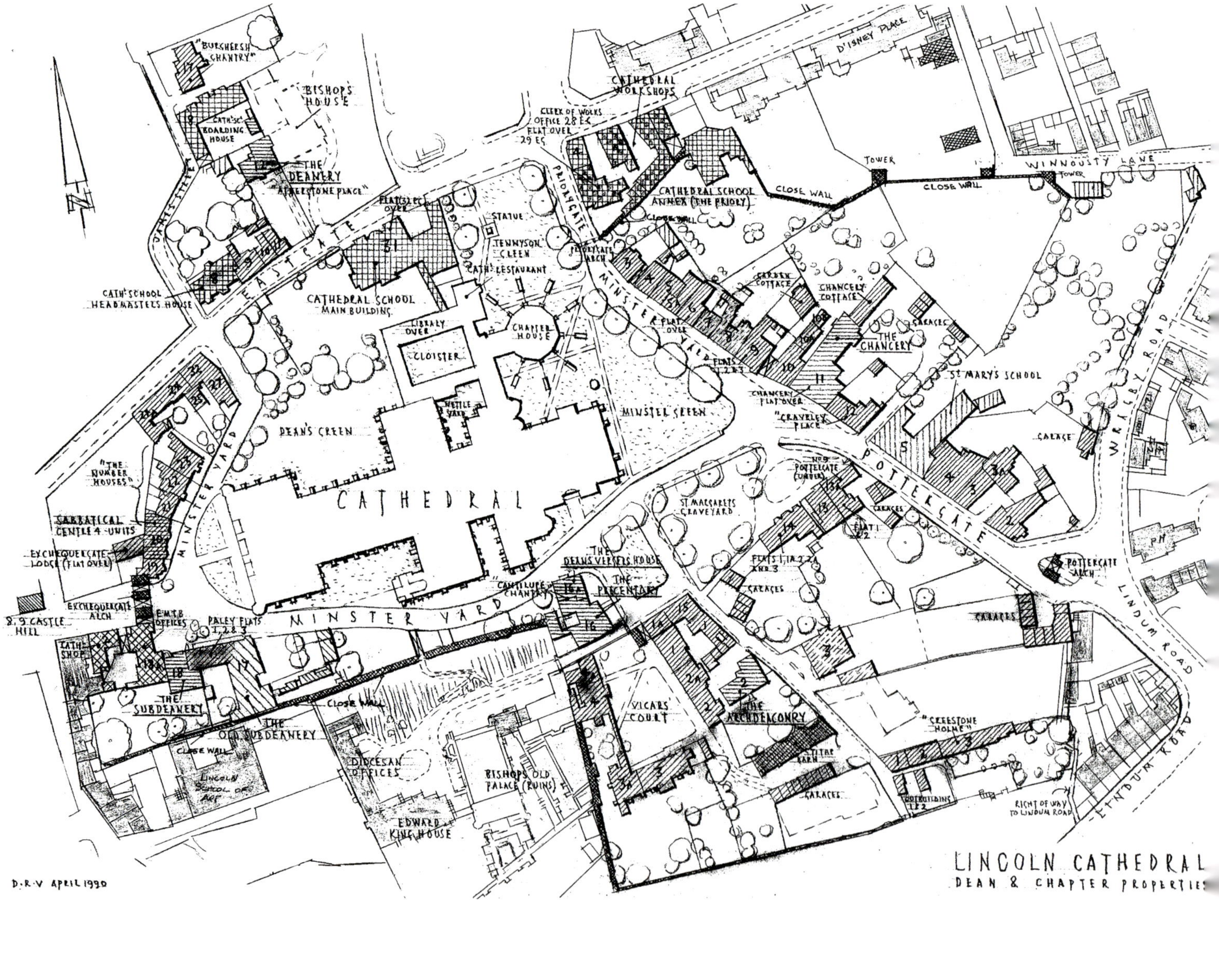

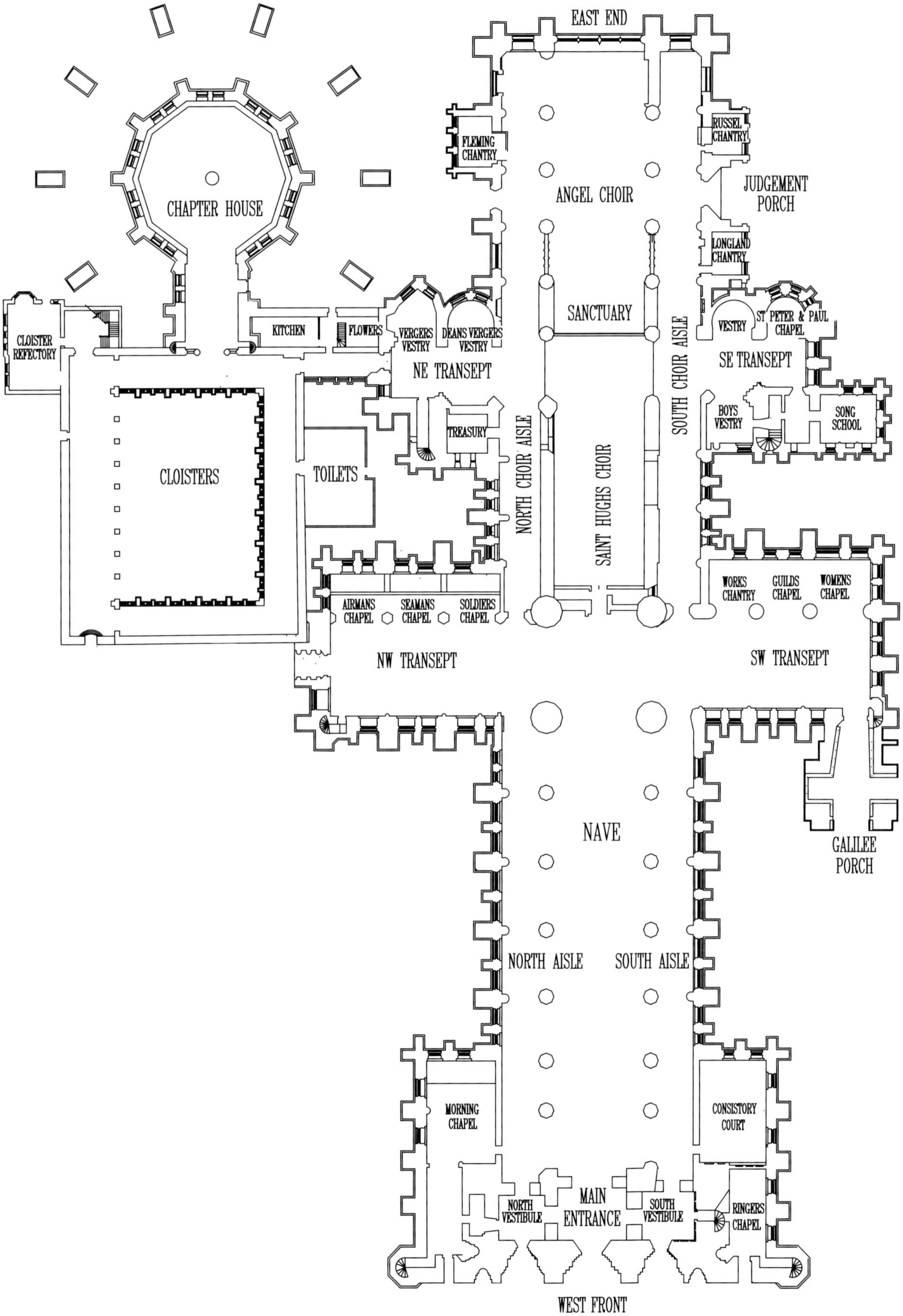
EAST END
CHAPTER HOUSE
FLEMING CHANTRY
RUSSEL CHANTRY
ANGEL CHOIR
JUDGEMENT PORCH
LONGLAND CHANTRY
SANCTUARY
CLOISTER REFECTORY
KITCHEN
FLOWERS
VERGERS VESTRY
DEANS VERGERS VESTRY
VESTRY
ST PETER & PAUL CHAPEL
NE TRANSEPT
SE TRANSEPT
SOUTH CHOIR AISLE
BOYS VESTRY
SONG SCHOOL
TREASURY
NORTH CHOIR AISLE
CLOISTERS
TOILETS
SAINT HUGHS CHOIR
WORKS CHANTRY
GUILDS CHAPEL
WOMENS CHAPEL
AIRMANS CHAPEL
SEAMANS CHAPEL
SOLDIERS CHAPEL
NW TRANSEPT
SW TRANSEPT
NAVE
GALILEE PORCH
NORTH AISLE
SOUTH AISLE
MORNING CHAPEL
CONSISTORY COURT
MAIN ENTRANCE
NORTH VESTIBULE
SOUTH VESTIBULE
RINGERS CHAPEL
WEST FRONT

LIST OF SUBSCRIBERS

Mrs Jean Ali
Mrs Gillian Anderson
Gwyneth and Richard Archer
Paul Arden
Sadie, Ffion and Euan Ashton-Lee
Gina Ashton
Paul and Lesley Ashton
Roy and Erica Astley
Mr R D Atkinson
Stephen K Bailey
Mrs Margaret A Baird MBE
Dr Jenny Baker-Weldon
Derek Latham Ballantyne
The Venerable T R Barker
Chris Barlow
L W Barnett
Susan M Barsley
Pamela Mary Bate
Mr Geoffrey Battle
Janet and Brian Beardsell
Caroline Mary Beckett
E Beckett
Ralph Beckingham OAM
Robert J Bell
Dr Nicholas Bennett
Roy and Sylvia Bentham
Zsuzsanna Bényei-Büttner
Mrs Patricia J Berrey
Mr John Beswick
Anne Binns
Mr Paul R Birchall
Dean Bird
Nigel Bird
Dawn and Jacqui Blanchard
Andrew Blow
Miss Maureen Blow
Peter Blow
Sheila and Norman Bonner
Thomas Brennan
Paul D Brewster
Mrs Sheila Brindley
Francis and Violet Brinkley
Edward Broughton
Bishop John Brown
Kenneth Brown
Pat Brown
His Honour Judge Robert Alan Brown
Matthew S I Bruce
The Dean of Lincoln and Mrs Philip Buckler
Susannah Buckler
Mrs Judith E Buckthorp
P and C Bunn
Trevor H Bush
Mr Teän and Mrs Heather Butcher
Mrs A M Camamile
Nevile and Lisa Camamile
J, P and P Campbell
Mr R Carroll Preston
Timothy J Carson
Mrs V M Chaffe
M G Chambers
Brent Charlesworth
Harriet Cheshire
Jean M Clark
Joseph John and Beryl Clark
Mrs Audrey Clarke
Mrs Eleanor Clarke
Ian Clarkson
John W A Clugston
John Cockett
Charles and Anne Coltman
Graham and Margaret Cook
Margaret Cook
Dennis Cooper
Sarah, Stephen and Emily Cooper
Marian A Corbett
Marguerite Corringham
Nigel and Harry Corringham
Charles W Coulsey
Keith Coulson
David Cowell
David J Cox
Jason and Sally Crawford
Janet Margaret Crawley
Robyn Crosby
C S Cullimore CBE OStJ DL
Rosemary Cumberland
Patrick and Ros Curbishley
Fiona and Jamie Curtis
Mr Richard Curtis
Doris Cuthbert
Mrs C M Dale
Tony Dallman
Alan Daniels
Mr Andrew and Mrs Elizabeth Dano
David J Davies
Mrs J Davies
Baroness Willoughby de Eresby
Adelbert Denaux, Dean, Tilburg School of Theology
Toby Dixon-Teasdale
Tristan Dixon-Teasdale
Bruce C Doggett
Revd Julie Donn

Mr G Douglas
Dr Steven Douglas
Jill Downs
R Dowson
Dr D J Drew
Mr R M Driver
Mrs P B Duce
Dr P Dunstan
Colin East
Hannah East
Liz East
Mr J E Lowday
Mrs S E Edwards
Mr and Mrs A Ellis
Valerie Elwell
Simon Erskine Crum
Mr and Mrs G Esam
Family Espejo-Mendiwelso
Dr David W Eveling
John I Eyres
Mr and Mrs Julian Fane
Andrew F J Farmer
Dr Georg Fexer and Susanne Fexer-Linder
Gillian Teresa Fiddes
Mrs Peggy Fisk
A J and C H G Flintham
Mr P E Forman
Mr and Mrs P Forrest
Zara Fountain
Christopher Frame
Patricia Frazer-Hollins
The Revd Canon J Freebairn-Smith
Lesley Freestone
Sandra and John Furst
Dr R C C Fynes
Mr Tony Gadd
Mr H W Gardiner
Mr and Mrs J K Gardiner
Andrew James Garner
Mrs Shirley Gaunt
Miss Maureen Claire Geddis
Mrs A K G German
Mrs P G Gill
The Gilmartin Family
Mrs M A Gleave
Carolyn Goddard
Frances Godden
Freda E Goodhead
Judith Gorst
Dr Steven and Mrs Barbara Goulden
Alan Goulding
Nicola Gracey
The Right Revd Alec Graham
Mrs Sandra Gratrick
Sir Michael Graydon
Mrs A Griffith
Mrs W R Groves
Peter and Janice Gull
Dorothy G Halfhide
C Robin Hall
Harold John Kemp Hall
Gillian Halliwell
Richard E Hanwell
Grace M Hardwick
Jeanette and Robert Hardwick
Colin Hare and Katie Hare
John Harley
Dr Richard Harper-Smith
Mrs Joyce Harris
Andrew J Harrison
Paul L Harrison
Mr George Hart
Mrs Margaret Hart
Mr R D Harvey
R and N Hawkins
Sheila Dawn Hay
Dr R C E Hayes
Carol M Heidschuster
Dr Neill and Julia Hepburn
Carol and Paul Hill
Jessie Hill
Candia Hillier
Simeon J D Hillier (Lincoln Cathedral Chorister 1987-93)
Tristram C E Hillier (Lincoln Cathedral Chorister 1985-8)
Mike Hills
Tobias Hinchliffe
Mr and Mrs R J Hirst
Douglas C Hoare
Roger Hobby
Marigold Hodgkinson
Canon Stephen Holdaway
James Holdsworth
Lesley and Ken Hollamby
Averil and Bryon Hollingworth
Ian Hollingworth
Miguel Holloway
Peggy Holloway
Barry Hopewell
Mr R C Horsley
Debbie and Richard Houston
Julie and Morris Howe
Charles Hull

The Revd Graham Hullett
Anne and Tom Hunter
Dr Joanna Huntington
Roy and Mary Ison
The Very Revd Brandon D Jackson
Robert A Jackson
T A Jaehrig
Jane Jagger
Mr D H P James
Jean James
Kathleen Jefferson
C J Jenkins
Cedric Jennings
Guy Johnson
K D Johnson
Miles and Gillian Jolly
Dilys Jones
Mike and Barbara Jones
Robert A Jones
Neville R M Kay TD FRCS
John and Emily Kearsey
Miss Michelle Keen
Mrs F C Kelly
Mr I F Kelly
Mr K F Kelly
Mrs Carolyn Kendall
Robert Kendrick
J R Kennedy
Patrick Kennedy
William Bruce Kennedy
Lyn Kenward
John Kinch
Ms J B King
Stuart King
John Kinton
The Revd Canon Gavin Kirk
J O Kirk
Rosemary Kirk
Maude Kitchen
The Very Reverend Alec and Mrs Sheelagh Knight
Betty N Knight
Mrs Jennifer Kuhnel
Alistair Laird
Mrs Pauline Laird
Flight Lieutenant R L C Lasham DFC and BAR
Nicholas Laurie
Mrs Hazel Lawson
Mrs J S Leach
Dr and Mrs C Leakey
Nigel and Janet Leaney
The Very Reverend David Leaning
Jane Leavesley
K M Ledgard
Lieutenant Commander The Revd A Donald Lee CD
John R Lester
Kenneth Lidbetter
Keith and Rosemary Lindop
Mrs Wendy Lloyd
J W Lockwood Esq.
Michael Loftus
Andrew P Long
Revd F and Mrs S Long
Charlie Longhorn
Tom Longhorn
John T Looke
Mr P E Lowis
Adrian Lucas and Family
Charles Lucas and Family
Michael Lucas and Family
Mrs Patricia Ann Mabbott
I H Macalpine-Leny
Gavin and Elizabeth Mackay
J T and V Macnaughton-Jones
Sylvia M Malt
Mrs A J Marchant
Market Rasen French Twinning Association
Mr and Mrs R Marnie
Leonard Marsh
Ann Teasdale Martin
Fr Edward Martin
Dorothy Mason
Freda Matassa
David and Christobel Mattingley
Edward Mayor
Dale McClain
V McQuaid
Mrs V J Meechan
Mr Keith Howard Melley
Mrs Patricia Mellows
Mrs Dorothy Middleton
Mr G A and Mrs C A Miles
Mrs Ieuan Miles
Richard and Anne Mills
Robert Mills
James Milne (Server)
S Scott Milne (Burghersh Chanter)
Stuart Milne (Burghersh Chanter)
Lord and Lady Monson
P Montgomery
His Honour Judge Ebraham Mooncey
Mr and Mrs Edward J Moore

Geoffrey Moore
John Moore
Michael D Moore
Mrs Valerie Moore
Richard Morley
Peter Morris
Lorraine Morrison
Matthew Morrissey
Mrs D Moss
George and Eileen Moulds
Peter and Deborah Mullins
Atle Naess
Michael Newstead
Mr Lyndon G Nicholas
Mary Nightingale
The Revd Canon Alan Nugent
Emily B M O'Reilly
Toni-Sandra Oliver
Joan and Terry Onyon
Revd and Mrs D J Osbourne
Mrs Helen E Page
Mr and Mrs M Paige
Joan Panton
Dr J R Parker
Jane Parker
Patricia A Parker
Mrs Ruth Parker, Lay Canon
The Revd Canon John Patrick
Revd Paul and Mrs Ruth Paynton
Elizabeth Peacock
Dr Ronald Pearce
S W and A Perchal
Valerie Perry
Chantal and Niru Philip
Frank and Micky Philp
Malcolm Phipps
Anthony W Pickard
Miss O M C Pogson
Mrs Margaret Pond
Ann J Porter
Roger Potter
Carole L Prescott (née Huntingford)
Clifford Price
Diana Price and Family
Mrs J L Price
Mrs Ruth Price
Reginald and Joan Priestley
Anne and Mike Pringle
John and Jean Proud
The Revd John and Mrs Sheila Pryor
Paul Pumfrey
Mrs Anita Quigley
Dr Keith Ramsay
Nicholas Rank
P H Raspin
Glennis Rathie
Mrs C E Richards
Shirley A Richardson
Nick Ridout
Dorothy May Rigby
John A Roberts FRIBA
David Robinson OBE
Mabel Rollin
Dick Rooke
Dr David Roper and Mrs Valerie Roper
Steve Rowan
Mrs A Elizabeth Rowe
Revd Peter A Rowe
Mr F J Rowley
James Ruscoe
The Revd Canon Neil Russell
Frank and Audrey Ryan
Ernest and Pauline Rylatt
Jean A Sacker
Marjorie E Salmon
Mrs M Sargeant
Roger K Saville
The Right Reverend Dr John Saxbee,
Bishop of Lincoln
Geoffrey Scard
Sally Scarfe
Mrs Monica Scorer
Eileen Scott
Graham and Janet Searston
Eileen Elizabeth Seddon
Mr R L Sellers
Sandra and Richard Sendall
Bryan J Seymour
E Sharp
Mrs Carolyn J Shaw
Jane E Shone
David Shucksmith
The Revd Canon Ian Geoffrey Silk
Revd Canon M and Mrs M Silley
Margaret Skipworth
Ian S Smart
Brian W Smith
P and S A Smith
Robert and Judith Smith
Mrs Elaine Smyth
Mr Robert Smyth
Garry and Lynn Snelson
Christopher John Sorby
Barrie and Judith Spark
Barbara R Spurrier

Rita Stancer
Dr Terence Stanford
The Revd Canon Terry Steele
Sheila M Stevens
David Stocker
R T Stokes
W L Stone
Shirley Stoneham
Edward Strange
Mr Adrian F Sunman
A Suttle
Peter Swann
Lord Taylor of Holbeach CBE
The Reverend Brian Taylor FSA
Brian and Christine Taylor
Pearl Taylor
Ursula and Hugh Taylor
Margaret Thomas
Anne Thompson
Dennis Thompson
Dr M E Thompson
Mr Sydney Thompson
Sheila Deebank Thornley
Cynthia Tinsley
Mrs Margaret Tointon
Maxine and Steve Tomashefsky
The Revd Jean M Tomlinson
Marilyn and Bob Tompkins
Mrs A Topliss
Mark D Tring
Richard Trudeau
Mrs Bea Tucker
Mrs June M Tucker
Revd D F Tunbridge BA HCF
Arthur Turner
Ian J Tyler
Mrs Barbara Varlow
Mrs Elys M Varney
Val Ventham
Adam Vero
Antony Vickers
D T Vigar
Stephen Vogt
Jeffrey Vollans
Dr Nikki Waddie, Lay Canon
Miss Sophie-Dominique Waddie
Miss E T Wagstaffe
Mrs Jean Waite
E Helen Walker
Eleanor and Alexander Walker
A D M Wallace-Cook
Mrs Diane Wallhead
William Wallis 1907-73
Mrs Helen Walsh
Arthur and Ann-Marie Ward
Captain T G S Ward
Sue Ware
Peter W Watkins
Ruby Eve Watkinson
Derek Wellman
Mrs Rosemary Wheeler
Mr A E W White
The Revd Canon M A Whitehead and
Mrs J D Whitehead
Ros Whitehead
Keith and Elaine Whitesides
Mr Mervyn and Mrs Margaret Whiting
Steve and Anne Wild
Dr R M Williams
John Williamson
David Willson
David and Elizabeth Wilson
Mrs E Wilson
Mrs J Wilson
M J Wilson and K McLean-Mair
Marianne Louise Wilson
Mr R G Winchester
Heather Winder
Revd Canon Kathryn Windslow
Bill Winterton, with loving memory
from his family
The Wipperman Family
Andrew Wood
Derek and Maureen Wood
Ernest Wood
Helen Wood
Mrs Pam Wood JP
K Woods
Loraine Woolley
David James Woolsey
Mr Tony Worth
Barbara M Wright
Neil and Sarah Wright
Mr T H Wright
Kevin and Jo Wynn
Erik Zindel

INDEX

Italics denotes image
Bold denotes author / contributor

Picture Credits

Phil Crow Front and back jacket, 2–3, 4, 6–7, 8, 11, 14, 17, 19(B), 43, 55(T), 56, 58(TL), 72, 73(B), 76(T), 86(T), 87(BL, TR), 89(R), 103,105,114, 123(R), 127, 132, 134–5, 136, 138(L), 139(ALL), 140(ALL), 141(ALL), 142, 143 (ALL), 144(TL, L, TR), 145, 146(L), 147(T), 148(TL,TR), 150(ALL), 151, 154–5

Dick Makin 9, 10, 12–13, 19(T), 20(ALL), 21, 23, 25, 26, 27(ALL), 28–9, 36 (ALL), 37, 38(B), 39(B), 41, 45, 48, 49, 50, 52, 54(ALL), 55, 57, 59(ALL), 61, (Greg Williams) 63, 65, 66(ALL), 67(ALL), 68(T), 69(TR), 70, 71, 73(L), 74(ALL), 75(B,B), 77(TR,R,BR), 78, 79, 80, 83, 85(ALL), 86(ALL), 87(R,TL), 88, 89(L), 90(L), 91,92(TR, R),93, 94(T), 95(TR,R,BR), 96, 97, 98, 99, 100,102,104,106,108, 109(Centre T, Centre B), 111, 112,113(T), 117,118(T),119,121(ALL), 122, 124,126,128, 129,130, 131, 138(R), 147(B), 149(ALL),157

Lincoln Cathedral Archives 11,18, 21, 28(T), 29(R), (David Lavash) 30–1, (Greg Williams) 33, (David Hayes) 35, 38(T), 39(T and INSET), 42(BL), (Gus de Cozar) 44, 47, 51, 53, (Dr Mike Lewins) 59, 68(BL, BR), 69(ALL), 72(INSET), 73(TR), 77(TL), 81, 82(ALL), 84(ALL), 89(TL), (Jo Turner) 90(B), 92(TR,TL), 94(B), 101, 103(B),107(TL,BL,TR, BL) ,110, 112, 113(INSET), 115(ALL), 116, 117,118(INSET), 119, 120(ALL), 121(ALL), 122(ALL), 123(L), 125, 127, 133(TL TR), 137, 147(B), 152, 153(ALL), 156, 158(L)

David Vale 32, 46, 62, 64(TR), 92(BL)

Other sources Courtesy John Bennett, www.lightanddreamsphotography.com 15; The Collection, Lincoln 16; Alamy 24; Getty Images 34, 95; *The Lincolnshire Echo* 60, 148(BL); Susan Pugsley 158(R)

Lincoln Cathedral: A Journey from Past to Present

First published in 2010 by
Third Millennium Publishing Limited,
a subsidiary of Third Millennium Information Limited.

2–5 Benjamin Street
London
United Kingdom
EC1M 5QL
www.tmiltd.com

ISBN 978 1 906507 19 0 (hardback)
ISBN 978 1 906507 20 6 (paperback)

Edited by Pamela Hartshorne
Designed by Susan Pugsley
Production by Bonnie Murray
Reprographics by Studio Fasoli, Italy
Printed by Printer Trento, Italy

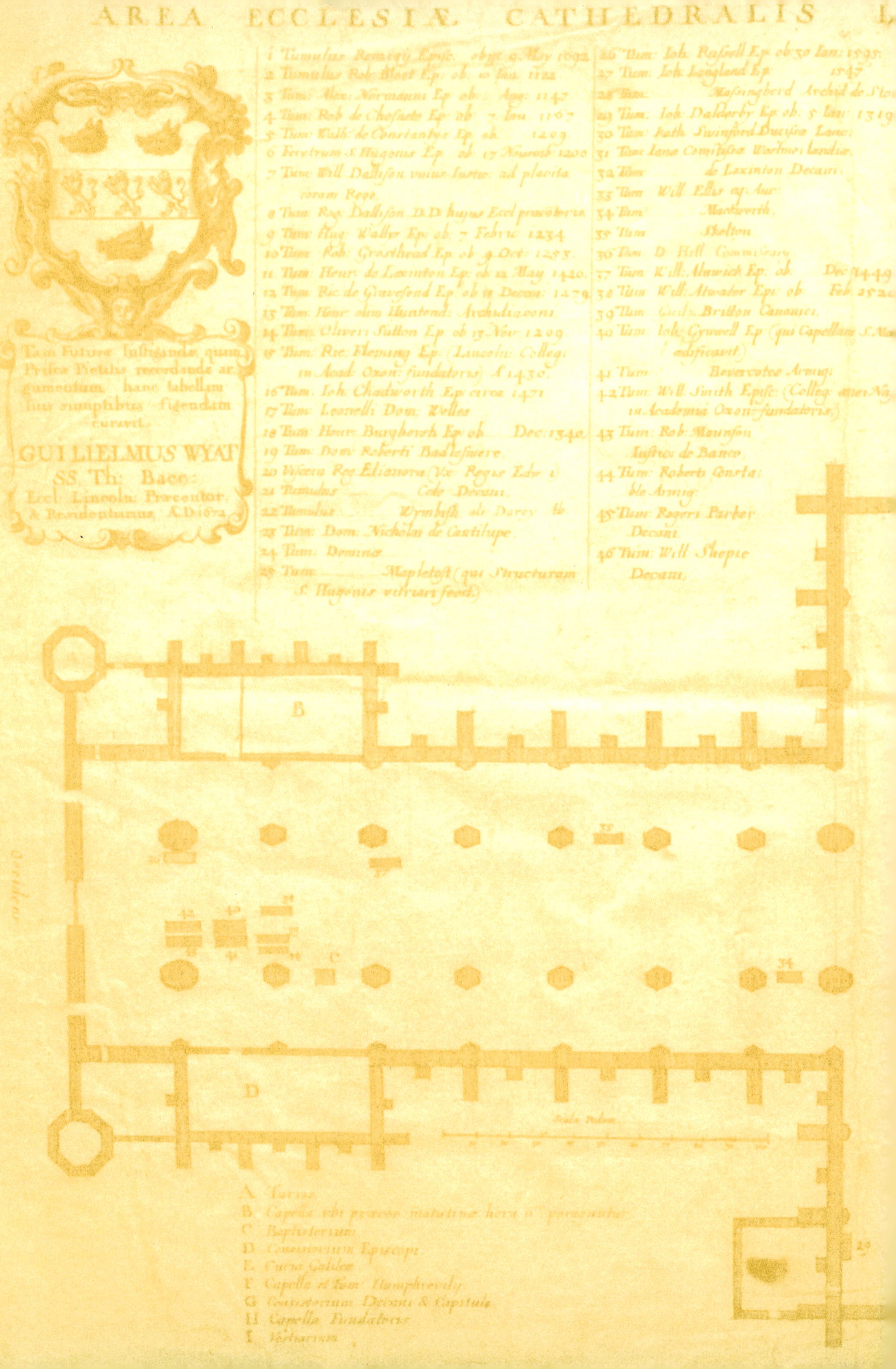
AREA ECCLESIÆ CATHEDRALIS L
1 Tumulus Remigij Episc. obijt 9 May 1092
2 Tumulus Rob: Bloet Ep: ob: 10 Ian. 1122
3 Tum: Alex: Normanni Ep ob: Aug: 1147
4 Tum: Rob de Chesneto Ep ob 7 Ian 1167
5 Tum: Walt: de Constantijs Ep ob 1209
6 Feretrum S. Hugonis Ep ob 17 Novemb: 1200
7 Tum: Will Dallison vnius Iustic: ad placita coram Rege.
8 Tum: Rog. Dallison D.D. huius Eccl praecentoris.
9 Tum: Hug: Waller Ep: ob 7 Febru: 1234
10 Tum: Rob: Grosthead Ep ob 9 Oct: 1253.
11 Tum: Henr: de Lexinton Ep: ob 22 May 1420.
12 Tum: Ric. de Gravesend Ep: ob 18 Decem: 1279.
13 Tum: Henr: olim Huntend: Archidiaconi.
14 Tum: Oliveri Sutton Ep ob 13 Nov: 1209.
15 Tum: Ric. Fleming Ep: (Lincoln: Colleg: in Acad: Oxon: fundatoris) A 1430.
16 Tum. Ioh. Chadworth Ep: circa 1471
17 Tum: Leonelli Dom: Welles
18 Tum: Henr: Burghersh Ep: ob Dec: 1340.
19 Tum: Dom: Roberti Badlesmere.
20 Viscera Reg. Elianora (Vx: Regis Edw 1)
21 Tumulus Cole Decani.
22 Tumulus Wymbish als Darcy
23 Tum: Dom: Nicholai de Cantilupe.
24 Tum: Dominae
25 Tum: Mapletoft (qui Structuram S. Hugonis vitriari fecit.)
26 Tum: Ioh: Russell Ep ob 30 Ian: 1595.
27 Tum: Ioh: Longland Ep 1547
28 Tum: Massingberd Archid de Sto
29 Tum: Ioh: Dalderby Ep: ob. 5 Ian: 1319
30 Tum: Kath: Swinford Ducissæ Lanc:
31 Tum: Ianæ Comitissæ Westmorlandiæ.
32 Tum: de Lexinton Decani.
33 Tum Will: Ellis eq: Aur:
34 Tum Mackworth.
35 Tum Shelton
36 Tum D. Hill Commissary.
37 Tum Will: Alnwick Ep: ob Dec 1449
38 Tum Will: Atwater Epi: ob Feb 1520
39 Tum Brillon Canonici.
40 Tum: Ioh: Gynwell Ep (qui Capellam S. Ma aedificavit)
41 Tum Bevercotes Armig:
42 Tum: Will Smith Episc: (Colleg: aenei Na in Academia Oxon: fundatoris)
43 Tum: Rob: Maunson Iustic: de Banco
44 Tum: Roberti Consta: ble Armig:
45 Tum: Rogeri Parker Decani
46 Tum: Will Shepie Decani.
Tam Futuræ Instigandæ quam Priscæ Pietatis recordandæ argumentum hanc tabellam suis sumptibus figendam curavit.
GUILIELMUS WYAT
SS. Th: Bacc:
Eccl Lincoln: Præcentor, & Residentiarius. A.D. 1672
A
B
C
D
34
A Turris
B Capella ubi preces matutinæ hora 6 peraguntur
C Baptisterium
D Consistorium Episcopi
E Curia Galilea
F Capella et Tum: Humphrevily.
G Consistorium Decani & Capitule
H Capella Fundatoris
I Vestiarium